Faithful Pages:
Your Bible Journal Adventure

Faithful Pages —Copyright ©2024 by By The Bootstraps – Melissa Bowers

Published by UNITED HOUSE Publishing
All rights reserved. No portion of this book may be reproduced or shared in any form–electronic, printed, photocopied, recording, or by any information storage and retrieval system, without prior written permission from the publisher. The use of short quotations is permitted.

The Holy Bible, English Standard Version. ESV® Text Edition: 2016. Copyright ©
2001 by Crossway Bibles, a publishing ministry of Good News Publishers.

All quotations used are stated by Mark Driscoll of Trinity Church in Scottsdale, AZ.

ISBN: 978-1-952840-56-2
UNITED HOUSE Publishing
Waterford, Michigan
info@unitedhousepublishing.com
www.unitedhousepublishing.com

Cover Layout and Interior Design:
Melissa Bowers
Printed in the United States of America
2024—First Edition

SPECIAL SALES
Most UNITED HOUSE books are available at special quantity discounts when purchased in bulk by corporations, organizations, and special-interest groups. For information, please e-mail orders@unitedhousepublishing.com

This Notebook Belongs To:

_____

All Scripture is breathed out by God and profitable for teaching, for reproof, for correction, and for training in righteousness, that the man of God may be complete, equipped for every good work.
-2 Timothy 3:16-17

Journaling

Yearly Devotion Plan

January	February	March	April	May	June
01	01	01	01	01	01
02	02	02	02	02	02
03	03	03	03	03	03
04	04	04	04	04	04
05	05	05	05	05	05
06	06	06	06	06	06
07	07	07	07	07	07
08	08	08	08	08	08
09	09	09	09	09	09
10	10	10	10	10	10
11	11	11	11	11	11
12	12	12	12	12	12
13	13	13	13	13	13
14	14	14	14	14	14
15	15	15	15	15	15
16	16	16	16	16	16
17	17	17	17	17	17
18	18	18	18	18	18
19	19	19	19	19	19
20	20	20	20	20	20
21	21	21	21	21	21
22	22	22	22	22	22
23	23	23	23	23	23
24	24	24	24	24	24
25	25	25	25	25	25
26	26	26	26	26	26
27	27	27	27	27	27
28	28	28	28	28	28
29		29	29	29	29
30		30	30	30	30
31				31	

Yearly Devotion Plan

July	August	September	October	November	December
01	01	01	01	01	01
02	02	02	02	02	02
03	03	03	03	03	03
04	04	04	04	04	04
05	05	05	05	05	05
06	06	06	06	06	06
07	07	07	07	07	07
08	08	08	08	08	08
09	09	09	09	09	09
10	10	10	10	10	10
11	11	11	11	11	11
12	12	12	12	12	12
13	13	13	13	13	13
14	14	14	14	14	14
15	15	15	15	15	15
16	16	16	16	16	16
17	17	17	17	17	17
18	18	18	18	18	18
19	19	19	19	19	19
20	20	20	20	20	20
21	21	21	21	21	21
22	22	22	22	22	22
23	23	23	23	23	23
24	24	24	24	24	24
25	25	25	25	25	25
26	26	26	26	26	26
27	27	27	27	27	27
28	28	28	28	28	28
29	29	29	29	29	29
30	30	30	30	30	30
31	31		31		31

Yearly Devotion Overview

January	February	March	April	May	June

July	August	September	October	November	December

How has God worked in your life this past year?
_____
_____
_____
_____
_____

What was the moment that reminded you of God's Greatness?
_____
_____
_____
_____
_____

What has God taught you this year?
_____
_____
_____
_____
_____

Scripture for the year:
_____
_____
_____
_____
_____

Bible Reading Tracker

The Law

Genesis
1 2 3 4 5
6 7 8 9 10
11 12 13 14 15
16 17 18 19 20
21 22 23 24 25
26 27 28 29 30
31 32 33 34 35
36 37 38 39 40
41 42 43 44 45
46 47 48 49 50

Exodus
1 2 3 4 5
6 7 8 9 10
11 12 13 14 15
16 17 18 19 20
21 22 23 24 25
26 27 28 29 30
31 32 33 34 35
36 37 38 39 40

Leviticus
1 2 3
4 5 6
7 8 9
10 11 12
13 14 15
16 17 18
19 20 21
22 23 24
25 26 27

Numbers
1 2 3 4
5 6 7 8
9 10 11 12
13 14 15 16
17 18 19 20
21 22 23 24
25 26 27 28
29 30 31 32
33 34 35 36

Deuteronomy
1 2 3 4 5
6 7 8 9 10
11 12 13 14 15
16 17 18 19 20
21 22 23 24 25
26 27 28 29 30
31 32 33 34

History

Joshua
1 2 3
4 5 6
7 8 9
10 11 12
13 14 15
16 17 18
19 20 21
22 23 24

Judges
1 2 3
4 5 6
7 8 9
10 11 12
13 14 15
16 17 18
19 20 21

Ruth
1 2
3 4

1 Samuel
1 2 3 4 5 6 7 8 9 10
11 12 13 14 15 16 17 18 19 20
21 22 23 24 25 26 27 28 29 30 31

2 Samuel
1 2 3 4 5 6 7 8
9 10 11 12 13 14 15 16
17 18 19 20 21 22 23 24

1 Kings
1 2 3
4 5 6
7 8 9
10 11 12
13 14 15
16 17 18
19 20 21
22

2 Kings
1 2 3 4
5 6 7 8
9 10 11 12
13 14 15 16
17 18 19 20
21 22 23 24
25

1 Chronicles
1 2 3 4 5
6 7 8 9 10
11 12 13 14 15
16 17 18 19 20
21 22 23 24 25
26 27 28 29

2 Chronicles
1 2 3 4 5 6
7 8 9 10 11 12
13 14 15 16 17 18
19 20 21 22 23 24
25 26 27 28 29 30
31 32 33 34 35 36

Ezra
1 2 3
4 5 6
7 8 9
10

Nehemiah
1 2 3 4 5 6 7
8 9 10 11 12 13

Esther
1 2 3 4
5 6 7 8
9 10

Bible Reading Tracker

Wisdom

Job
1, 2, 3, 4, 5, 6, 7, 8, 9, 10, 11, 12, 13, 14, 15, 16, 17, 18, 19, 20, 21, 22, 23, 24, 25, 26, 27, 28, 29, 30, 31, 32, 33, 34, 35, 36, 37, 38, 39, 40, 41, 42

Psalms
1–150

Proverbs
1–31

Ecclesiastes
1–12

Song of Solomon
1–8

Prophets

Isaiah
1–66

Jeremiah
1–52

Lamentations
1–5

Ezekiel
1–48

Daniel
1–12

Hosea
1–14

Joel
1–3

Obadiah
1

Amos
1–9

Jonah
1–4

Micah
1–7

Nahum
1–3

Habakkuk
1–3

Zephaniah
1–3

Haggai
1–2

Zechariah
1–14

Malachi
1–4

400 YEARS go by...

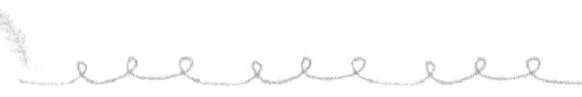

Bible Reading Tracker

January

"We open our Bibles to learn, we open our lives to love so that lives and legacies are transformed"
-Mark Driscoll

January

1. _____
2. _____
3. _____
4. _____
5. _____
6. _____
7. _____
8. _____
9. _____
10. _____
11. _____
12. _____
13. _____
14. _____
15. _____
16. _____
17. _____
18. _____
19. _____
20. _____
21. _____
22. _____
23. _____
24. _____
25. _____
26. _____
27. _____
28. _____
29. _____
30. _____
31. _____

Monthly Intention	Monthly Reflection
This month's prayer focus:	What I'm thankful for this month:
To make this month great I will:	What I have learned about God:
What I'm looking forward to this month:	Who I served this month:

Weekly Bible Goals/Faith In Action

Date: _____

Sunday	
Monday	
Tuesday	
Wednesday	
Thursday	
Friday	
Saturday	

IT'S ALL ABOUT JESUS

Weekly Reflection

Before I Start My Week:

What am I grateful for?

What does God want me to do this week?

What area do I want God to bless me?

How can I be Salt & Light to my community?

After My Week Ends:

How did I see God working in me?

Was I honoring God with my actions?

What things could I have done differently?

How did I reflect Christ's love this week?

Scripture Studied

Author:_____ Where:_____

When:_____ Why:_____

Scripture:

Cross Reverences::

Observation:

Application:

Notes:

IT'S ALL ABOUT JESUS

Summary of What I Learned

Important Locations:

Memory Verse

Key Words:

Questions:

Key People:

Weekly Prayer

My Prayer Focus:

My praise and worship

_____
_____
_____
_____

Lord I am grateful for...

_____
_____
_____
_____

Lord teach me to....

_____
_____
_____
_____

What are the struggles I am facing?

_____
_____
_____
_____

What may be God's answer to my prayer?

_____
_____
_____
_____

Prayer:

_____
_____
_____
_____
_____
_____
_____
_____
_____
_____
_____
_____
_____
_____
_____
_____
_____
_____
_____
_____
_____
_____
_____

IT'S ALL ABOUT JESUS

Weekly Revelation

How did the Lord speak to me?
_____
_____
_____
_____
_____

Discription of what I saw/heard:

How do I feel about this revelation?
_____
_____
_____
_____
_____

What may be the interpretation?
_____
_____
_____
_____
_____
_____
_____
_____
_____

Biblical References :
- _____
- _____
- _____
- _____
- _____

IT'S ALL ABOUT JESUS

Weekly Self-Reflection

Verse:_____ Topic:_____

What's the context?
_____
_____
_____

Similar Verses:
- _____
- _____
- _____
- _____
- _____
- _____

My initial thoughts:
_____
_____
_____
_____

What immediately stands out to me about this verse?
_____
_____
_____
_____

Does this show me how Christians are supposed to live?
_____
_____
_____
_____

Is there an example of this verse in the first 5 books of the Bible?
_____
_____
_____
_____

Does this remind me of anything Jesus said or did?
_____
_____
_____
_____

IT'S ALL ABOUT JESUS

Weekly Self-Reflection

Question I am pondering about today:

Self-Reflection Journal Prompts

1. What is God asking me to prioritize over the upcoming six months?
2. Today, God has given me someone to pray for.
3. Is my behavior this week indicating that I'm content with my life circumstances?
4. Who is God urging me to let go of my grudge against?
5. What aspects of the fruit of the Spirit do I need to enlist assistance in developing?
6. How can I help others by shining a light in a dark place?
7. Is there a time when I feel the most distant from the Lord?
8. How is my arrogance driving me to cause harm to others?
9. Do I find it difficult to communicate my regrets? If that's the case, why?
10. Choose a Biblical figure. What can I glean from their narrative?
11. What or who do I fear? Why?
12. How does God want me to listen to him?
13. What is the "next step" for my spiritual growth?
14. Am I pleasing God in my singleness/ married life/ as a parent?
15. Is there anything in my life that I should put my trust in the Lord for?
16. Describe the three most vulnerable areas of myself.
17. Describe three occasions in my life when the Lord provided for me and served as my protection.
18. According to Ecclesiastes, there is a season for everything. Which season am I now in?
19. Write my own Psalm of praise/thanksgiving to God.
20. When did Jesus Christ become my Lord and Savior?
21. How might I live within the anointing of the Lord?
22. Recall a period in my life when the Lord delivered me.
23. In my perspective, what will heaven be like?
24. What might I do this year to improve my patience?
25. How could I become more grateful this year?
26. Is it possible that I'm growing arrogant in some way? How can I make it right?
27. How can I make this year more enjoyable?
28. How can I make this year a more peaceful one for myself?
29. What could I do this year to cultivate obedience to the Lord?
30. How can I love more this year?
31. How can I become nicer and gentler this year?
32. Write a letter of forgiveness to an enemy.
33. If I am struggling with something, what do I think God wants me to learn from it?
34. What spiritual gifts do I possess? What can I do with them to further God's kingdom?
35. Write on a time when the Lord spoke to me.
36. Be still and listen. What is the Lord revealing to me at this moment?
37. When do I most strongly feel God's presence? What can I do when I don't feel His presence near?
38. The last time something angered me, how did I react to it? What does the reply reveal about my character?
39. How does my pride respond when something offends me?
40. How can I experience the Lord's healing in my life?
41. Who is one individual I can specifically help? How?
42. What steals my peace by diverting my thoughts from God?
43. When have I sensed God's grasp and presence lifting me up?
44. What component of my relationship with the Lord makes me the most thankful?
45. Which Bible scripture is my favorite, and why?
46. Do I just celebrate when things are going well? Can I celebrate while in famine?
47. What transgressions must I repent of to the Lord?
48. Make a list of song lyrics that speak to me and explain why.
49. What has been the greatest blessing so far in my life?
50. What am I sensing God calling me to change in my life?

IT'S ALL ABOUT JESUS

Weekly Bible Goals/Faith In Action

Date: _____

Sunday	
Monday	
Tuesday	
Wednesday	
Thursday	
Friday	
Saturday	

Weekly Reflection

Before I Start My Week:	After My Week Ends:
What am I grateful for?	How did I see God working in me?
What does God want me to do this week?	Was I honoring God with my actions?
What area do I want God to bless me?	What things could I have done differently?
How can I be Salt & Light to my community?	How did I reflect Christ's love this week?

IT'S ALL ABOUT JESUS

Scripture Studied

Author:_____ Where:_____

When:_____ Why:_____

Scripture:

_____
_____
_____
_____
_____

Cross Reverences::

_____
_____
_____
_____

Observation:

Application:

Notes:

_____
_____
_____
_____
_____
_____

Summary of What I Learned

_____
_____
_____
_____
_____

Important Locations:

Memory Verse
_____
_____
_____
_____
_____
_____
_____
_____
_____
_____
_____
_____
_____

Key Words:
- _____
- _____
- _____
- _____
- _____

Questions:
- _____
- _____
- _____
- _____
- _____

Key People:
- _____
- _____
- _____
- _____

IT'S ALL ABOUT JESUS

Weekly Prayer

My Prayer Focus:

My praise and worship

_____
_____
_____

Lord I am grateful for...

_____
_____
_____

Lord teach me to....

_____
_____
_____

What are the struggles I am facing?

_____
_____
_____

What may be God's answer to my prayer?

_____
_____
_____

Prayer:

_____
_____
_____
_____
_____
_____
_____
_____
_____
_____
_____
_____
_____
_____
_____
_____
_____
_____
_____
_____
_____
_____
_____
_____
_____

Weekly Revelation

How did the Lord speak to me?
_____
_____
_____
_____
_____

Discription of what I saw/heard:

How do I feel about this revelation?
_____
_____
_____
_____

What may be the interpretation?
_____
_____
_____
_____
_____
_____
_____

Biblical References:
- _____
- _____
- _____
- _____
- _____

IT'S ALL ABOUT JESUS

Weekly Self-Reflection

Verse:_____ Topic:_____

What's the context?

_____
_____
_____

My initial thoughts:

_____
_____
_____

Similar Verses :

- _____
- _____
- _____
- _____
- _____
- _____

What immediately stands out to me about this verse?

_____
_____
_____
_____

Does this show me how Christians are supposed to live?

_____
_____
_____
_____

Is there an example of this verse in the first 5 books of the Bible?

_____
_____
_____
_____

Does this remind me of anything Jesus said or did?

_____
_____
_____
_____

IT'S ALL ABOUT JESUS

Weekly Self-Reflection

Question I am pondering about today:

IT'S ALL ABOUT JESUS

Self-Reflection Journal Prompts

1. What is God asking me to prioritize over the upcoming six months?
2. Today, God has given me someone to pray for.
3. Is my behavior this week indicating that I'm content with my life circumstances?
4. Who is God urging me to let go of my grudge against?
5. What aspects of the fruit of the Spirit do I need to enlist assistance in developing?
6. How can I help others by shining a light in a dark place?
7. Is there a time when I feel the most distant from the Lord?
8. How is my arrogance driving me to cause harm to others?
9. Do I find it difficult to communicate my regrets? If that's the case, why?
10. Choose a Biblical figure. What can I glean from their narrative?
11. What or who do I fear? Why?
12. How does God want me to listen to him?
13. What is the "next step" for my spiritual growth?
14. Am I pleasing God in my singleness/ married life/ as a parent?
15. Is there anything in my life that I should put my trust in the Lord for?
16. Describe the three most vulnerable areas of myself.
17. Describe three occasions in my life when the Lord provided for me and served as my protection.
18. According to Ecclesiastes, there is a season for everything. Which season am I now in?
19. Write my own Psalm of praise/thanksgiving to God.
20. When did Jesus Christ become my Lord and Savior?
21. How might I live within the anointing of the Lord?
22. Recall a period in my life when the Lord delivered me.
23. In my perspective, what will heaven be like?
24. What might I do this year to improve my patience?
25. How could I become more grateful this year?
26. Is it possible that I'm growing arrogant in some way? How can I make it right?
27. How can I make this year more enjoyable?
28. How can I make this year a more peaceful one for myself?
29. What could I do this year to cultivate obedience to the Lord?
30. How can I love more this year?
31. How can I become nicer and gentler this year?
32. Write a letter of forgiveness to an enemy.
33. If I am struggling with something, what do I think God wants me to learn from it?
34. What spiritual gifts do I possess? What can I do with them to further God's kingdom?
35. Write on a time when the Lord spoke to me.
36. Be still and listen. What is the Lord revealing to me at this moment?
37. When do I most strongly feel God's presence? What can I do when I don't feel His presence near?
38. The last time something angered me, how did I react to it? What does the reply reveal about my character?
39. How does my pride respond when something offends me?
40. How can I experience the Lord's healing in my life?
41. Who is one individual I can specifically help? How?
42. What steals my peace by diverting my thoughts from God?
43. When have I sensed God's grasp and presence lifting me up?
44. What component of my relationship with the Lord makes me the most thankful?
45. Which Bible scripture is my favorite, and why?
46. Do I just celebrate when things are going well? Can I celebrate while in famine?
47. What transgressions must I repent of to the Lord?
48. Make a list of song lyrics that speak to me and explain why.
49. What has been the greatest blessing so far in my life?
50. What am I sensing God calling me to change in my life?

Weekly Bible Goals/Faith In Action

Date: _____

Sunday	
Monday	
Tuesday	
Wednesday	
Thursday	
Friday	
Saturday	

IT'S ALL ABOUT JESUS

Weekly Reflection

Before I Start My Week:	After My Week Ends:
What am I grateful for?	How did I see God working in me?
What does God want me to do this week?	Was I honoring God with my actions?
What area do I want God to bless me?	What things could I have done differently?
How can I be Salt & Light to my community?	How did I reflect Christ's love this week?

Scripture Studied

Author:_____ Where:_____

When:_____ Why:_____

Scripture:

Cross Reverences::

Observation:

Application:

Notes:

IT'S ALL ABOUT JESUS

Summary of What I Learned

Important Locations:

Memory Verse

Key Words:

Questions:

Key People:

Weekly Prayer

My Prayer Focus:

My praise and worship

_____
_____
_____
_____

Lord I am grateful for...

_____
_____
_____
_____

Lord teach me to....

_____
_____
_____
_____

What are the struggles I am facing?

_____
_____
_____
_____

What may be God's answer to my prayer?

_____
_____
_____
_____

Prayer:

_____
_____
_____
_____
_____
_____
_____
_____
_____
_____
_____
_____
_____
_____
_____
_____
_____
_____
_____
_____
_____
_____
_____
_____

IT'S ALL ABOUT JESUS

Weekly Revelation

How did the Lord speak to me?

Discription of what I saw/heard:

How do I feel about this revelation?

What may be the interpretation?

Biblical References:

- _____
- _____
- _____
- _____
- _____

IT'S ALL ABOUT JESUS

Weekly Self-Reflection

Verse:_____   Topic:_____

What's the context?   Similar Verses :
_____   • _____
_____   • _____
_____   • _____

My initial thoughts: • _____
_____   • _____
_____   • _____
_____

What immediately stands out to me about this verse?
_____
_____
_____
_____

Does this show me how Christians are supposed to live?
_____
_____
_____
_____

Is there an example of this verse in the first 5 books of the Bible?
_____
_____
_____
_____

Does this remind me of anything Jesus said or did?
_____
_____
_____
_____

IT'S ALL ABOUT JESUS

Weekly Self-Reflection

Question I am pondering about today:

Self-Reflection Journal Prompts

1. What is God asking me to prioritize over the upcoming six months?
2. Today, God has given me someone to pray for.
3. Is my behavior this week indicating that I'm content with my life circumstances?
4. Who is God urging me to let go of my grudge against?
5. What aspects of the fruit of the Spirit do I need to enlist assistance in developing?
6. How can I help others by shining a light in a dark place?
7. Is there a time when I feel the most distant from the Lord?
8. How is my arrogance driving me to cause harm to others?
9. Do I find it difficult to communicate my regrets? If that's the case, why?
10. Choose a Biblical figure. What can I glean from their narrative?
11. What or who do I fear? Why?
12. How does God want me to listen to him?
13. What is the "next step" for my spiritual growth?
14. Am I pleasing God in my singleness/ married life/ as a parent?
15. Is there anything in my life that I should put my trust in the Lord for?
16. Describe the three most vulnerable areas of myself.
17. Describe three occasions in my life when the Lord provided for me and served as my protection.
18. According to Ecclesiastes, there is a season for everything. Which season am I now in?
19. Write my own Psalm of praise/thanksgiving to God.
20. When did Jesus Christ become my Lord and Savior?
21. How might I live within the anointing of the Lord?
22. Recall a period in my life when the Lord delivered me.
23. In my perspective, what will heaven be like?
24. What might I do this year to improve my patience?
25. How could I become more grateful this year?
26. Is it possible that I'm growing arrogant in some way? How can I make it right?
27. How can I make this year more enjoyable?
28. How can I make this year a more peaceful one for myself?
29. What could I do this year to cultivate obedience to the Lord?
30. How can I love more this year?
31. How can I become nicer and gentler this year?
32. Write a letter of forgiveness to an enemy.
33. If I am struggling with something, what do I think God wants me to learn from it?
34. What spiritual gifts do I possess? What can I do with them to further God's kingdom?
35. Write on a time when the Lord spoke to me.
36. Be still and listen. What is the Lord revealing to me at this moment?
37. When do I most strongly feel God's presence? What can I do when I don't feel His presence near?
38. The last time something angered me, how did I react to it? What does the reply reveal about my character?
39. How does my pride respond when something offends me?
40. How can I experience the Lord's healing in my life?
41. Who is one individual I can specifically help? How?
42. What steals my peace by diverting my thoughts from God?
43. When have I sensed God's grasp and presence lifting me up?
44. What component of my relationship with the Lord makes me the most thankful?
45. Which Bible scripture is my favorite, and why?
46. Do I just celebrate when things are going well? Can I celebrate while in famine?
47. What transgressions must I repent of to the Lord?
48. Make a list of song lyrics that speak to me and explain why.
49. What has been the greatest blessing so far in my life?
50. What am I sensing God calling me to change in my life?

IT'S ALL ABOUT JESUS

Weekly Bible Goals/Faith In Action

Date: _____

Sunday	
Monday	
Tuesday	
Wednesday	
Thursday	
Friday	
Saturday	

Weekly Reflection

Before I Start My Week:

What am I grateful for?

What does God want me to do this week?

What area do I want God to bless me?

How can I be Salt & Light to my community?

After My Week Ends:

How did I see God working in me?

Was I honoring God with my actions?

What things could I have done differently?

How did I reflect Christ's love this week?

IT'S ALL ABOUT JESUS

Scripture Studied

Author:_____   Where:_____

When:_____   Why:_____

Scripture:

Cross Reverences::

Observation:

Application:

Notes:

Summary of What I Learned

Important Locations:

Memory Verse

Key Words:

Questions:

Key People:

IT'S ALL ABOUT JESUS

Weekly Prayer

My Prayer Focus:

My praise and worship

Lord I am grateful for...

Lord teach me to....

What are the struggles I am facing?

What may be God's answer to my prayer?

Prayer:

IT'S ALL ABOUT JESUS

Weekly Revelation

How did the Lord speak to me?

Discription of what I saw/heard:

How do I feel about this revelation?

What may be the interpretation?

- Biblical References :

IT'S ALL ABOUT JESUS

Weekly Self-Reflection

Verse:_____   Topic:_____

What's the context?

_____
_____
_____

My initial thoughts:

_____
_____
_____

Similar Verses:

- _____
- _____
- _____
- _____
- _____
- _____

What immediately stands out to me about this verse?

_____
_____
_____
_____

Does this show me how Christians are supposed to live?

_____
_____
_____
_____

Is there an example of this verse in the first 5 books of the Bible?

_____
_____
_____
_____

Does this remind me of anything Jesus said or did?

_____
_____
_____
_____

IT'S ALL ABOUT JESUS

Weekly Self-Reflection

Question I am pondering about today:

IT'S ALL ABOUT JESUS

Self-Reflection Journal Prompts

1. What is God asking me to prioritize over the upcoming six months?
2. Today, God has given me someone to pray for.
3. Is my behavior this week indicating that I'm content with my life circumstances?
4. Who is God urging me to let go of my grudge against?
5. What aspects of the fruit of the Spirit do I need to enlist assistance in developing?
6. How can I help others by shining a light in a dark place?
7. Is there a time when I feel the most distant from the Lord?
8. How is my arrogance driving me to cause harm to others?
9. Do I find it difficult to communicate my regrets? If that's the case, why?
10. Choose a Biblical figure. What can I glean from their narrative?
11. What or who do I fear? Why?
12. How does God want me to listen to him?
13. What is the "next step" for my spiritual growth?
14. Am I pleasing God in my singleness/ married life/ as a parent?
15. Is there anything in my life that I should put my trust in the Lord for?
16. Describe the three most vulnerable areas of myself.
17. Describe three occasions in my life when the Lord provided for me and served as my protection.
18. According to Ecclesiastes, there is a season for everything. Which season am I now in?
19. Write my own Psalm of praise/thanksgiving to God.
20. When did Jesus Christ become my Lord and Savior?
21. How might I live within the anointing of the Lord?
22. Recall a period in my life when the Lord delivered me.
23. In my perspective, what will heaven be like?
24. What might I do this year to improve my patience?
25. How could I become more grateful this year?
26. Is it possible that I'm growing arrogant in some way? How can I make it right?
27. How can I make this year more enjoyable?
28. How can I make this year a more peaceful one for myself?
29. What could I do this year to cultivate obedience to the Lord?
30. How can I love more this year?
31. How can I become nicer and gentler this year?
32. Write a letter of forgiveness to an enemy.
33. If I am struggling with something, what do I think God wants me to learn from it?
34. What spiritual gifts do I possess? What can I do with them to further God's kingdom?
35. Write on a time when the Lord spoke to me.
36. Be still and listen. What is the Lord revealing to me at this moment?
37. When do I most strongly feel God's presence? What can I do when I don't feel His presence near?
38. The last time something angered me, how did I react to it? What does the reply reveal about my character?
39. How does my pride respond when something offends me?
40. How can I experience the Lord's healing in my life?
41. Who is one individual I can specifically help? How?
42. What steals my peace by diverting my thoughts from God?
43. When have I sensed God's grasp and presence lifting me up?
44. What component of my relationship with the Lord makes me the most thankful?
45. Which Bible scripture is my favorite, and why?
46. Do I just celebrate when things are going well? Can I celebrate while in famine?
47. What transgressions must I repent of to the Lord?
48. Make a list of song lyrics that speak to me and explain why.
49. What has been the greatest blessing so far in my life?
50. What am I sensing God calling me to change in my life?

February

"To get a word <u>from</u> God, we need to open up the Word <u>of</u> God"
-Mark Driscoll

February

1. _____
2. _____
3. _____
4. _____
5. _____
6. _____
7. _____
8. _____
9. _____
10. _____
11. _____
12. _____
13. _____
14. _____
15. _____
16. _____
17. _____
18. _____
19. _____
20. _____
21. _____
22. _____
23. _____
24. _____
25. _____
26. _____
27. _____
28. _____
29. _____

Monthly Intention	Monthly Reflection
This month's prayer focus:	What I'm thankful for this month:
To make this month great I will:	What I have learned about God:
What I'm looking forward to this month:	Who I served this month:

Weekly Bible Goals/Faith In Action

Date: _____

Sunday	
Monday	
Tuesday	
Wednesday	
Thursday	
Friday	
Saturday	

IT'S ALL ABOUT JESUS

Weekly Reflection

Before I Start My Week:	After My Week Ends:
What am I grateful for?	How did I see God working in me?
What does God want me to do this week?	Was I honoring God with my actions?
What area do I want God to bless me?	What things could I have done differently?
How can I be Salt & Light to my community?	How did I reflect Christ's love this week?

IT'S ALL ABOUT JESUS

Scripture Studied

Author:_____   Where:_____

When:_____   Why:_____

Scripture:
_____
_____
_____
_____
_____
_____
_____

Cross Reverences::
_____
_____
_____
_____

Observation:

Application:

Notes:
_____
_____
_____
_____
_____
_____

IT'S ALL ABOUT JESUS

Summary of What I Learned

Important Locations:

Memory Verse

Key Words:

Questions:

Key People:

Weekly Prayer

My Prayer Focus:

My praise and worship

_____
_____
_____
_____

Lord I am grateful for...

_____
_____
_____
_____

Lord teach me to....

_____
_____
_____
_____

What are the struggles I am facing?

_____
_____
_____
_____

What may be God's answer to my prayer?

_____
_____
_____
_____

Prayer:

_____
_____
_____
_____
_____
_____
_____
_____
_____
_____
_____
_____
_____
_____
_____
_____
_____
_____
_____
_____

IT'S ALL ABOUT JESUS

Weekly Revelation

How did the Lord speak to me?
_____
_____
_____
_____
_____

Discription of what I saw/heard:

How do I feel about this revelation?
_____
_____
_____
_____
_____
_____

What may be the interpretation?
_____
_____
_____
_____
_____
_____
_____
_____
_____
_____
_____

Biblical References:
- _____
- _____
- _____
- _____
- _____

IT'S ALL ABOUT JESUS

Weekly Self-Reflection

Verse:_____   Topic:_____

What's the context?
_____
_____
_____

Similar Verses:
- _____
- _____
- _____
- _____
- _____
- _____

My initial thoughts:
_____
_____
_____

What immediately stands out to me about this verse?
_____
_____
_____
_____

Does this show me how Christians are supposed to live?
_____
_____
_____
_____

Is there an example of this verse in the first 5 books of the Bible?
_____
_____
_____
_____

Does this remind me of anything Jesus said or did?
_____
_____
_____
_____

IT'S ALL ABOUT JESUS

Weekly Self-Reflection

Question I am pondering about today:

Self-Reflection Journal Prompts

1. What is God asking me to prioritize over the upcoming six months?
2. Today, God has given me someone to pray for.
3. Is my behavior this week indicating that I'm content with my life circumstances?
4. Who is God urging me to let go of my grudge against?
5. What aspects of the fruit of the Spirit do I need to enlist assistance in developing?
6. How can I help others by shining a light in a dark place?
7. Is there a time when I feel the most distant from the Lord?
8. How is my arrogance driving me to cause harm to others?
9. Do I find it difficult to communicate my regrets? If that's the case, why?
10. Choose a Biblical figure. What can I glean from their narrative?
11. What or who do I fear? Why?
12. How does God want me to listen to him?
13. What is the "next step" for my spiritual growth?
14. Am I pleasing God in my singleness/ married life/ as a parent?
15. Is there anything in my life that I should put my trust in the Lord for?
16. Describe the three most vulnerable areas of myself.
17. Describe three occasions in my life when the Lord provided for me and served as my protection.
18. According to Ecclesiastes, there is a season for everything. Which season am I now in?
19. Write my own Psalm of praise/thanksgiving to God.
20. When did Jesus Christ become my Lord and Savior?
21. How might I live within the anointing of the Lord?
22. Recall a period in my life when the Lord delivered me.
23. In my perspective, what will heaven be like?
24. What might I do this year to improve my patience?
25. How could I become more grateful this year?
26. Is it possible that I'm growing arrogant in some way? How can I make it right?
27. How can I make this year more enjoyable?
28. How can I make this year a more peaceful one for myself?
29. What could I do this year to cultivate obedience to the Lord?
30. How can I love more this year?
31. How can I become nicer and gentler this year?
32. Write a letter of forgiveness to an enemy.
33. If I am struggling with something, what do I think God wants me to learn from it?
34. What spiritual gifts do I possess? What can I do with them to further God's kingdom?
35. Write on a time when the Lord spoke to me.
36. Be still and listen. What is the Lord revealing to me at this moment?
37. When do I most strongly feel God's presence? What can I do when I don't feel His presence near?
38. The last time something angered me, how did I react to it? What does the reply reveal about my character?
39. How does my pride respond when something offends me?
40. How can I experience the Lord's healing in my life?
41. Who is one individual I can specifically help? How?
42. What steals my peace by diverting my thoughts from God?
43. When have I sensed God's grasp and presence lifting me up?
44. What component of my relationship with the Lord makes me the most thankful?
45. Which Bible scripture is my favorite, and why?
46. Do I just celebrate when things are going well? Can I celebrate while in famine?
47. What transgressions must I repent of to the Lord?
48. Make a list of song lyrics that speak to me and explain why.
49. What has been the greatest blessing so far in my life?
50. What am I sensing God calling me to change in my life?

IT'S ALL ABOUT JESUS

Weekly Bible Goals/Faith In Action

Date: _____

Sunday	
Monday	
Tuesday	
Wednesday	
Thursday	
Friday	
Saturday	

IT'S ALL ABOUT JESUS

Weekly Reflection

Before I Start My Week:	After My Week Ends:
What am I grateful for?	How did I see God working in me?
What does God want me to do this week?	Was I honoring God with my actions?
What area do I want God to bless me?	What things could I have done differently?
How can I be Salt & Light to my community?	How did I reflect Christ's love this week?

IT'S ALL ABOUT JESUS

Scripture Studied

Author:_____   Where:_____

When:_____   Why:_____

Scripture:

Cross Reverences::

Observation:

Application:

Notes:

Summary of What I Learned

Important Locations:

Memory Verse

Key Words:

Questions:

Key People:

IT'S ALL ABOUT JESUS

Weekly Prayer

My Prayer Focus:

My praise and worship
_____
_____
_____
_____

Lord I am grateful for...
_____
_____
_____
_____

Lord teach me to....
_____
_____
_____
_____

What are the struggles I am facing?
_____
_____
_____
_____

What may be God's answer to my prayer?
_____
_____
_____
_____

Prayer:
_____
_____
_____
_____
_____
_____
_____
_____
_____
_____
_____
_____
_____
_____
_____
_____
_____
_____
_____
_____

IT'S ALL ABOUT JESUS

Weekly Revelation

How did the Lord speak to me?
_____
_____
_____
_____
_____

Discription of what I saw/heard:

How do I feel about this revelation?
_____
_____
_____
_____
_____
_____
_____

What may be the interpretation?
_____
_____
_____
_____
_____
_____
_____
_____
_____
_____
_____
_____

Biblical References:
- _____
- _____
- _____
- _____
- _____

IT'S ALL ABOUT JESUS

Weekly Self-Reflection

Verse:_____   Topic:_____

What's the context?
_____
_____
_____
_____

My initial thoughts:
_____
_____
_____
_____

Similar Verses:
- _____
- _____
- _____
- _____
- _____
- _____

What immediately stands out to me about this verse?
_____
_____
_____
_____
_____

Does this show me how Christians are supposed to live?
_____
_____
_____
_____
_____

Is there an example of this verse in the first 5 books of the Bible?
_____
_____
_____
_____

Does this remind me of anything Jesus said or did?
_____
_____
_____
_____

Weekly Self-Reflection

Question I am pondering about today:

IT'S ALL ABOUT JESUS

Self-Reflection Journal Prompts

1. What is God asking me to prioritize over the upcoming six months?
2. Today, God has given me someone to pray for.
3. Is my behavior this week indicating that I'm content with my life circumstances?
4. Who is God urging me to let go of my grudge against?
5. What aspects of the fruit of the Spirit do I need to enlist assistance in developing?
6. How can I help others by shining a light in a dark place?
7. Is there a time when I feel the most distant from the Lord?
8. How is my arrogance driving me to cause harm to others?
9. Do I find it difficult to communicate my regrets? If that's the case, why?
10. Choose a Biblical figure. What can I glean from their narrative?
11. What or who do I fear? Why?
12. How does God want me to listen to him?
13. What is the "next step" for my spiritual growth?
14. Am I pleasing God in my singleness/ married life/ as a parent?
15. Is there anything in my life that I should put my trust in the Lord for?
16. Describe the three most vulnerable areas of myself.
17. Describe three occasions in my life when the Lord provided for me and served as my protection.
18. According to Ecclesiastes, there is a season for everything. Which season am I now in?
19. Write my own Psalm of praise/thanksgiving to God.
20. When did Jesus Christ become my Lord and Savior?
21. How might I live within the anointing of the Lord?
22. Recall a period in my life when the Lord delivered me.
23. In my perspective, what will heaven be like?
24. What might I do this year to improve my patience?
25. How could I become more grateful this year?
26. Is it possible that I'm growing arrogant in some way? How can I make it right?
27. How can I make this year more enjoyable?
28. How can I make this year a more peaceful one for myself?
29. What could I do this year to cultivate obedience to the Lord?
30. How can I love more this year?
31. How can I become nicer and gentler this year?
32. Write a letter of forgiveness to an enemy.
33. If I am struggling with something, what do I think God wants me to learn from it?
34. What spiritual gifts do I possess? What can I do with them to further God's kingdom?
35. Write on a time when the Lord spoke to me.
36. Be still and listen. What is the Lord revealing to me at this moment?
37. When do I most strongly feel God's presence? What can I do when I don't feel His presence near?
38. The last time something angered me, how did I react to it? What does the reply reveal about my character?
39. How does my pride respond when something offends me?
40. How can I experience the Lord's healing in my life?
41. Who is one individual I can specifically help? How?
42. What steals my peace by diverting my thoughts from God?
43. When have I sensed God's grasp and presence lifting me up?
44. What component of my relationship with the Lord makes me the most thankful?
45. Which Bible scripture is my favorite, and why?
46. Do I just celebrate when things are going well? Can I celebrate while in famine?
47. What transgressions must I repent of to the Lord?
48. Make a list of song lyrics that speak to me and explain why.
49. What has been the greatest blessing so far in my life?
50. What am I sensing God calling me to change in my life?

Weekly Bible Goals/Faith In Action

Date: _____

Sunday	
Monday	
Tuesday	
Wednesday	
Thursday	
Friday	
Saturday	

IT'S ALL ABOUT JESUS

Weekly Reflection

Before I Start My Week:

What am I grateful for?

What does God want me to do this week?

What area do I want God to bless me?

How can I be Salt & Light to my community?

After My Week Ends:

How did I see God working in me?

Was I honoring God with my actions?

What things could I have done differently?

How did I reflect Christ's love this week?

IT'S ALL ABOUT JESUS

Scripture Studied

Author:_____   Where:_____

When:_____   Why:_____

Scripture:

Cross Reverences::

Observation:

Application:

Notes:

IT'S ALL ABOUT JESUS

Summary of What I Learned

Important Locations:

Memory Verse

Key Words:

Questions:

Key People:

It's All About Jesus

Weekly Prayer

My Prayer Focus:

My praise and worship

_____
_____
_____
_____

Lord I am grateful for...

_____
_____
_____
_____

Lord teach me to....

_____
_____
_____
_____

What are the struggles I am facing?

_____
_____
_____
_____

What may be God's answer to my prayer?

_____
_____
_____
_____

Prayer:

_____
_____
_____
_____
_____
_____
_____
_____
_____
_____
_____
_____
_____
_____
_____
_____
_____
_____
_____
_____
_____
_____
_____
_____
_____
_____
_____

IT'S ALL ABOUT JESUS

Weekly Revelation

How did the Lord speak to me?
_____
_____
_____
_____
_____

Discription of what I saw/heard:

How do I feel about this revelation?
_____
_____
_____
_____
_____
_____

What may be the interpretation?
_____
_____
_____
_____
_____
_____
_____
_____
_____
_____

Biblical References :
- _____
- _____
- _____
- _____
- _____

IT'S ALL ABOUT JESUS

Weekly Self-Reflection

Verse:_____   Topic:_____

What's the context?

_____
_____
_____

My initial thoughts:

_____
_____
_____

Similar Verses:
- _____
- _____
- _____
- _____
- _____
- _____

What immediately stands out to me about this verse?

_____
_____
_____
_____

Does this show me how Christians are supposed to live?

_____
_____
_____
_____

Is there an example of this verse in the first 5 books of the Bible?

_____
_____
_____
_____

Does this remind me of anything Jesus said or did?

_____
_____
_____
_____

IT'S ALL ABOUT JESUS

Weekly Self-Reflection

Question I am pondering about today:

Self-Reflection Journal Prompts

1. What is God asking me to prioritize over the upcoming six months?
2. Today, God has given me someone to pray for.
3. Is my behavior this week indicating that I'm content with my life circumstances?
4. Who is God urging me to let go of my grudge against?
5. What aspects of the fruit of the Spirit do I need to enlist assistance in developing?
6. How can I help others by shining a light in a dark place?
7. Is there a time when I feel the most distant from the Lord?
8. How is my arrogance driving me to cause harm to others?
9. Do I find it difficult to communicate my regrets? If that's the case, why?
10. Choose a Biblical figure. What can I glean from their narrative?
11. What or who do I fear? Why?
12. How does God want me to listen to him?
13. What is the "next step" for my spiritual growth?
14. Am I pleasing God in my singleness/ married life/ as a parent?
15. Is there anything in my life that I should put my trust in the Lord for?
16. Describe the three most vulnerable areas of myself.
17. Describe three occasions in my life when the Lord provided for me and served as my protection.
18. According to Ecclesiastes, there is a season for everything. Which season am I now in?
19. Write my own Psalm of praise/thanksgiving to God.
20. When did Jesus Christ become my Lord and Savior?
21. How might I live within the anointing of the Lord?
22. Recall a period in my life when the Lord delivered me.
23. In my perspective, what will heaven be like?
24. What might I do this year to improve my patience?
25. How could I become more grateful this year?
26. Is it possible that I'm growing arrogant in some way? How can I make it right?
27. How can I make this year more enjoyable?
28. How can I make this year a more peaceful one for myself?
29. What could I do this year to cultivate obedience to the Lord?
30. How can I love more this year?
31. How can I become nicer and gentler this year?
32. Write a letter of forgiveness to an enemy.
33. If I am struggling with something, what do I think God wants me to learn from it?
34. What spiritual gifts do I possess? What can I do with them to further God's kingdom?
35. Write on a time when the Lord spoke to me.
36. Be still and listen. What is the Lord revealing to me at this moment?
37. When do I most strongly feel God's presence? What can I do when I don't feel His presence near?
38. The last time something angered me, how did I react to it? What does the reply reveal about my character?
39. How does my pride respond when something offends me?
40. How can I experience the Lord's healing in my life?
41. Who is one individual I can specifically help? How?
42. What steals my peace by diverting my thoughts from God?
43. When have I sensed God's grasp and presence lifting me up?
44. What component of my relationship with the Lord makes me the most thankful?
45. Which Bible scripture is my favorite, and why?
46. Do I just celebrate when things are going well? Can I celebrate while in famine?
47. What transgressions must I repent of to the Lord?
48. Make a list of song lyrics that speak to me and explain why.
49. What has been the greatest blessing so far in my life?
50. What am I sensing God calling me to change in my life?

IT'S ALL ABOUT JESUS

Weekly Bible Goals/Faith In Action

Date: _____

Day	
Sunday	
Monday	
Tuesday	
Wednesday	
Thursday	
Friday	
Saturday	

Weekly Reflection

Before I Start My Week:

What am I grateful for?

What does God want me to do this week?

What area do I want God to bless me?

How can I be Salt & Light to my community?

After My Week Ends:

How did I see God working in me?

Was I honoring God with my actions?

What things could I have done differently?

How did I reflect Christ's love this week?

IT'S ALL ABOUT JESUS

Scripture Studied

Author:_____   Where:_____

When:_____   Why:_____

Scripture:

_____
_____
_____
_____
_____

Cross Reverences::

_____
_____
_____
_____

Observation:

Application:

Notes:

_____
_____
_____
_____
_____

IT'S ALL ABOUT JESUS

Summary of What I Learned

Important Locations:

Memory Verse

Key Words:

Questions:

Key People:

IT'S ALL ABOUT JESUS

Weekly Prayer

My Prayer Focus:

My praise and worship

_____
_____
_____
_____

Lord I am grateful for...

_____
_____
_____
_____

Lord teach me to....

_____
_____
_____
_____

What are the struggles I am facing?

_____
_____
_____
_____

What may be God's answer to my prayer?

_____
_____
_____
_____

Prayer:

_____
_____
_____
_____
_____
_____
_____
_____
_____
_____
_____
_____
_____
_____
_____
_____
_____
_____
_____
_____
_____
_____
_____
_____

Weekly Revelation

How did the Lord speak to me?
_____
_____
_____
_____
_____

Discription of what I saw/heard:

How do I feel about this revelation?
_____
_____
_____
_____
_____
_____

What may be the interpretation?
_____
_____
_____
_____
_____
_____
_____
_____
_____

Biblical References :
- _____
- _____
- _____
- _____
- _____

IT'S ALL ABOUT JESUS

Weekly Self-Reflection

Verse:_____ Topic:_____

What's the context?
_____
_____
_____

Similar Verses :
- _____
- _____
- _____
- _____
- _____
- _____

My initial thoughts:
_____
_____
_____

What immediately stands out to me about this verse?
_____
_____
_____
_____

Does this show me how Christians are supposed to live?
_____
_____
_____
_____

Is there an example of this verse in the first 5 books of the Bible?
_____
_____
_____
_____

Does this remind me of anything Jesus said or did?
_____
_____
_____
_____

IT'S ALL ABOUT JESUS

Weekly Self-Reflection

Question I am pondering about today:

IT'S ALL ABOUT JESUS

Self-Reflection Journal Prompts

1. What is God asking me to prioritize over the upcoming six months?
2. Today, God has given me someone to pray for.
3. Is my behavior this week indicating that I'm content with my life circumstances?
4. Who is God urging me to let go of my grudge against?
5. What aspects of the fruit of the Spirit do I need to enlist assistance in developing?
6. How can I help others by shining a light in a dark place?
7. Is there a time when I feel the most distant from the Lord?
8. How is my arrogance driving me to cause harm to others?
9. Do I find it difficult to communicate my regrets? If that's the case, why?
10. Choose a Biblical figure. What can I glean from their narrative?
11. What or who do I fear? Why?
12. How does God want me to listen to him?
13. What is the "next step" for my spiritual growth?
14. Am I pleasing God in my singleness/ married life/ as a parent?
15. Is there anything in my life that I should put my trust in the Lord for?
16. Describe the three most vulnerable areas of myself.
17. Describe three occasions in my life when the Lord provided for me and served as my protection.
18. According to Ecclesiastes, there is a season for everything. Which season am I now in?
19. Write my own Psalm of praise/thanksgiving to God.
20. When did Jesus Christ become my Lord and Savior?
21. How might I live within the anointing of the Lord?
22. Recall a period in my life when the Lord delivered me.
23. In my perspective, what will heaven be like?
24. What might I do this year to improve my patience?
25. How could I become more grateful this year?
26. Is it possible that I'm growing arrogant in some way? How can I make it right?
27. How can I make this year more enjoyable?
28. How can I make this year a more peaceful one for myself?
29. What could I do this year to cultivate obedience to the Lord?
30. How can I love more this year?
31. How can I become nicer and gentler this year?
32. Write a letter of forgiveness to an enemy.
33. If I am struggling with something, what do I think God wants me to learn from it?
34. What spiritual gifts do I possess? What can I do with them to further God's kingdom?
35. Write on a time when the Lord spoke to me.
36. Be still and listen. What is the Lord revealing to me at this moment?
37. When do I most strongly feel God's presence? What can I do when I don't feel His presence near?
38. The last time something angered me, how did I react to it? What does the reply reveal about my character?
39. How does my pride respond when something offends me?
40. How can I experience the Lord's healing in my life?
41. Who is one individual I can specifically help? How?
42. What steals my peace by diverting my thoughts from God?
43. When have I sensed God's grasp and presence lifting me up?
44. What component of my relationship with the Lord makes me the most thankful?
45. Which Bible scripture is my favorite, and why?
46. Do I just celebrate when things are going well? Can I celebrate while in famine?
47. What transgressions must I repent of to the Lord?
48. Make a list of song lyrics that speak to me and explain why.
49. What has been the greatest blessing so far in my life?
50. What am I sensing God calling me to change in my life?

March

"The Bible is a weapon. Not for beating people up with your theology, but for cutting to the core of the issues we deal with in this very dark world. It is our weapon of war, and it's not for the faint of heart."
-Mark Driscoll

March

1. _____
2. _____
3. _____
4. _____
5. _____
6. _____
7. _____
8. _____
9. _____
10. _____
11. _____
12. _____
13. _____
14. _____
15. _____
16. _____
17. _____
18. _____
19. _____
20. _____
21. _____
22. _____
23. _____
24. _____
25. _____
26. _____
27. _____
28. _____
29. _____
30. _____
31. _____

Monthly Intention	Monthly Reflection
This month's prayer focus:	What I'm thankful for this month:
To make this month great I will:	What I have learned about God:
What I'm looking forward to this month:	Who I served this month:

Weekly Bible Goals/Faith In Action

Date: _____

Sunday	
Monday	
Tuesday	
Wednesday	
Thursday	
Friday	
Saturday	

IT'S ALL ABOUT JESUS

Weekly Reflection

Before I Start My Week:	After My Week Ends:
What am I grateful for?	How did I see God working in me?
What does God want me to do this week?	Was I honoring God with my actions?
What area do I want God to bless me?	What things could I have done differently?
How can I be Salt & Light to my community?	How did I reflect Christ's love this week?

Scripture Studied

Author:_____   Where:_____

When:_____   Why:_____

Scripture:

Cross Reverences::

Observation:

Application:

Notes:

IT'S ALL ABOUT JESUS

Summary of What I Learned

Important Locations:

Memory Verse

Key Words:
-
-
-
-
-

Questions:
-
-
-
-
-
-

Key People:
-
-
-
-

Weekly Prayer

My Prayer Focus:

My praise and worship

_____
_____
_____
_____

Lord I am grateful for...

_____
_____
_____
_____

Lord teach me to....

_____
_____
_____
_____

What are the struggles I am facing?

_____
_____
_____
_____

What may be God's answer to my prayer?

_____
_____
_____
_____

Prayer:

_____
_____
_____
_____
_____
_____
_____
_____
_____
_____
_____
_____
_____
_____
_____
_____
_____
_____
_____
_____
_____
_____
_____
_____
_____
_____
_____
_____

IT'S ALL ABOUT JESUS

Weekly Revelation

How did the Lord speak to me?
_____
_____
_____
_____

Discription of what I saw/heard:

How do I feel about this revelation?
_____
_____
_____
_____
_____

What may be the interpretation?
_____
_____
_____
_____
_____
_____
_____
_____

Biblical References :
- _____
- _____
- _____
- _____
- _____

IT'S ALL ABOUT JESUS

Weekly Self-Reflection

Verse:_____ Topic:_____

What's the context?

_____
_____
_____

My initial thoughts:

_____
_____
_____

Similar Verses:
- _____
- _____
- _____
- _____
- _____
- _____

What immediately stands out to me about this verse?

_____
_____
_____
_____

Does this show me how Christians are supposed to live?

_____
_____
_____
_____

Is there an example of this verse in the first 5 books of the Bible?

_____
_____
_____
_____

Does this remind me of anything Jesus said or did?

_____
_____
_____
_____

IT'S ALL ABOUT JESUS

Weekly Self-Reflection

Question I am pondering about today:

Self-Reflection Journal Prompts

1. What is God asking me to prioritize over the upcoming six months?
2. Today, God has given me someone to pray for.
3. Is my behavior this week indicating that I'm content with my life circumstances?
4. Who is God urging me to let go of my grudge against?
5. What aspects of the fruit of the Spirit do I need to enlist assistance in developing?
6. How can I help others by shining a light in a dark place?
7. Is there a time when I feel the most distant from the Lord?
8. How is my arrogance driving me to cause harm to others?
9. Do I find it difficult to communicate my regrets? If that's the case, why?
10. Choose a Biblical figure. What can I glean from their narrative?
11. What or who do I fear? Why?
12. How does God want me to listen to him?
13. What is the "next step" for my spiritual growth?
14. Am I pleasing God in my singleness/ married life/ as a parent?
15. Is there anything in my life that I should put my trust in the Lord for?
16. Describe the three most vulnerable areas of myself.
17. Describe three occasions in my life when the Lord provided for me and served as my protection.
18. According to Ecclesiastes, there is a season for everything. Which season am I now in?
19. Write my own Psalm of praise/thanksgiving to God.
20. When did Jesus Christ become my Lord and Savior?
21. How might I live within the anointing of the Lord?
22. Recall a period in my life when the Lord delivered me.
23. In my perspective, what will heaven be like?
24. What might I do this year to improve my patience?
25. How could I become more grateful this year?
26. Is it possible that I'm growing arrogant in some way? How can I make it right?
27. How can I make this year more enjoyable?
28. How can I make this year a more peaceful one for myself?
29. What could I do this year to cultivate obedience to the Lord?
30. How can I love more this year?
31. How can I become nicer and gentler this year?
32. Write a letter of forgiveness to an enemy.
33. If I am struggling with something, what do I think God wants me to learn from it?
34. What spiritual gifts do I possess? What can I do with them to further God's kingdom?
35. Write on a time when the Lord spoke to me.
36. Be still and listen. What is the Lord revealing to me at this moment?
37. When do I most strongly feel God's presence? What can I do when I don't feel His presence near?
38. The last time something angered me, how did I react to it? What does the reply reveal about my character?
39. How does my pride respond when something offends me?
40. How can I experience the Lord's healing in my life?
41. Who is one individual I can specifically help? How?
42. What steals my peace by diverting my thoughts from God?
43. When have I sensed God's grasp and presence lifting me up?
44. What component of my relationship with the Lord makes me the most thankful?
45. Which Bible scripture is my favorite, and why?
46. Do I just celebrate when things are going well? Can I celebrate while in famine?
47. What transgressions must I repent of to the Lord?
48. Make a list of song lyrics that speak to me and explain why.
49. What has been the greatest blessing so far in my life?
50. What am I sensing God calling me to change in my life?

IT'S ALL ABOUT JESUS

Weekly Bible Goals/Faith In Action

Date: _____

Day	
Sunday	
Monday	
Tuesday	
Wednesday	
Thursday	
Friday	
Saturday	

Weekly Reflection

Before I Start My Week:	After My Week Ends:
What am I grateful for?	How did I see God working in me?
What does God want me to do this week?	Was I honoring God with my actions?
What area do I want God to bless me?	What things could I have done differently?
How can I be Salt & Light to my community?	How did I reflect Christ's love this week?

IT'S ALL ABOUT JESUS

Scripture Studied

Author:_____   Where:_____

When:_____   Why:_____

Scripture:

Cross Reverences::

Observation:

Application:

Notes:

Summary of What I Learned

Important Locations:

Memory Verse

Key Words:

Questions:

Key People:

IT'S ALL ABOUT JESUS

Weekly Prayer

My Prayer Focus:

My praise and worship

Lord I am grateful for...

Lord teach me to....

What are the struggles I am facing?

What may be God's answer to my prayer?

Prayer:

Weekly Revelation

How did the Lord speak to me?
_____
_____
_____
_____

Discription of what I saw/heard:

How do I feel about this revelation?
_____
_____
_____
_____
_____
_____

What may be the interpretation?
_____
_____
_____
_____
_____
_____
_____
_____
_____

Biblical References:
- _____
- _____
- _____
- _____
- _____

IT'S ALL ABOUT JESUS

Weekly Self-Reflection

Verse:_____ Topic:_____

What's the context?
_____
_____
_____

My initial thoughts:
_____
_____
_____

Similar Verses:
- _____
- _____
- _____
- _____
- _____
- _____

What immediately stands out to me about this verse?
_____
_____
_____
_____

Does this show me how Christians are supposed to live?
_____
_____
_____
_____

Is there an example of this verse in the first 5 books of the Bible?
_____
_____
_____
_____

Does this remind me of anything Jesus said or did?
_____
_____
_____
_____

IT'S ALL ABOUT JESUS

Weekly Self-Reflection

Question I am pondering about today:

IT'S ALL ABOUT JESUS

Self-Reflection Journal Prompts

1. What is God asking me to prioritize over the upcoming six months?
2. Today, God has given me someone to pray for.
3. Is my behavior this week indicating that I'm content with my life circumstances?
4. Who is God urging me to let go of my grudge against?
5. What aspects of the fruit of the Spirit do I need to enlist assistance in developing?
6. How can I help others by shining a light in a dark place?
7. Is there a time when I feel the most distant from the Lord?
8. How is my arrogance driving me to cause harm to others?
9. Do I find it difficult to communicate my regrets? If that's the case, why?
10. Choose a Biblical figure. What can I glean from their narrative?
11. What or who do I fear? Why?
12. How does God want me to listen to him?
13. What is the "next step" for my spiritual growth?
14. Am I pleasing God in my singleness/ married life/ as a parent?
15. Is there anything in my life that I should put my trust in the Lord for?
16. Describe the three most vulnerable areas of myself.
17. Describe three occasions in my life when the Lord provided for me and served as my protection.
18. According to Ecclesiastes, there is a season for everything. Which season am I now in?
19. Write my own Psalm of praise/thanksgiving to God.
20. When did Jesus Christ become my Lord and Savior?
21. How might I live within the anointing of the Lord?
22. Recall a period in my life when the Lord delivered me.
23. In my perspective, what will heaven be like?
24. What might I do this year to improve my patience?
25. How could I become more grateful this year?
26. Is it possible that I'm growing arrogant in some way? How can I make it right?
27. How can I make this year more enjoyable?
28. How can I make this year a more peaceful one for myself?
29. What could I do this year to cultivate obedience to the Lord?
30. How can I love more this year?
31. How can I become nicer and gentler this year?
32. Write a letter of forgiveness to an enemy.
33. If I am struggling with something, what do I think God wants me to learn from it?
34. What spiritual gifts do I possess? What can I do with them to further God's kingdom?
35. Write on a time when the Lord spoke to me.
36. Be still and listen. What is the Lord revealing to me at this moment?
37. When do I most strongly feel God's presence? What can I do when I don't feel His presence near?
38. The last time something angered me, how did I react to it? What does the reply reveal about my character?
39. How does my pride respond when something offends me?
40. How can I experience the Lord's healing in my life?
41. Who is one individual I can specifically help? How?
42. What steals my peace by diverting my thoughts from God?
43. When have I sensed God's grasp and presence lifting me up?
44. What component of my relationship with the Lord makes me the most thankful?
45. Which Bible scripture is my favorite, and why?
46. Do I just celebrate when things are going well? Can I celebrate while in famine?
47. What transgressions must I repent of to the Lord?
48. Make a list of song lyrics that speak to me and explain why.
49. What has been the greatest blessing so far in my life?
50. What am I sensing God calling me to change in my life?

IT'S ALL ABOUT JESUS

Weekly Bible Goals/Faith In Action

Date: _____

Sunday	
Monday	
Tuesday	
Wednesday	
Thursday	
Friday	
Saturday	

IT'S ALL ABOUT JESUS

Weekly Reflection

Before I Start My Week:

What am I grateful for?

What does God want me to do this week?

What area do I want God to bless me?

How can I be Salt & Light to my community?

After My Week Ends:

How did I see God working in me?

Was I honoring God with my actions?

What things could I have done differently?

How did I reflect Christ's love this week?

IT'S ALL ABOUT JESUS

Scripture Studied

Author:_____ Where:_____

When:_____ Why:_____

Scripture:

Cross Reverences::

Observation:

Application:

Notes:
_____
_____
_____
_____
_____

IT'S ALL ABOUT JESUS

Summary of What I Learned

Important Locations:

Memory Verse

Key Words:
-
-
-
-
-

Questions:
-
-
-
-
-

Key People:
-
-
-
-

IT'S ALL ABOUT JESUS

Weekly Prayer

My Prayer Focus:

My praise and worship

_____
_____
_____
_____

Lord I am grateful for...

_____
_____
_____
_____

Lord teach me to....

_____
_____
_____
_____

What are the struggles I am facing?

_____
_____
_____
_____

What may be God's answer to my prayer?

_____
_____
_____
_____

Prayer:

_____
_____
_____
_____
_____
_____
_____
_____
_____
_____
_____
_____
_____
_____
_____
_____
_____
_____
_____
_____
_____
_____
_____
_____

IT'S ALL ABOUT JESUS

Weekly Revelation

How did the Lord speak to me?

Discription of what I saw/heard:

How do I feel about this revelation?

What may be the interpretation?

Biblical References:

- _____
- _____
- _____
- _____
- _____

Weekly Self-Reflection

Verse:_____   Topic:_____

What's the context?
_____
_____
_____

My initial thoughts:
_____
_____
_____
_____

Similar Verses:
- _____
- _____
- _____
- _____
- _____
- _____

What immediately stands out to me about this verse?
_____
_____
_____
_____

Does this show me how Christians are supposed to live?
_____
_____
_____
_____

Is there an example of this verse in the first 5 books of the Bible?
_____
_____
_____
_____

Does this remind me of anything Jesus said or did?
_____
_____
_____
_____

IT'S ALL ABOUT JESUS

Weekly Self-Reflection

Question I am pondering about today:

Self-Reflection Journal Prompts

1. What is God asking me to prioritize over the upcoming six months?
2. Today, God has given me someone to pray for.
3. Is my behavior this week indicating that I'm content with my life circumstances?
4. Who is God urging me to let go of my grudge against?
5. What aspects of the fruit of the Spirit do I need to enlist assistance in developing?
6. How can I help others by shining a light in a dark place?
7. Is there a time when I feel the most distant from the Lord?
8. How is my arrogance driving me to cause harm to others?
9. Do I find it difficult to communicate my regrets? If that's the case, why?
10. Choose a Biblical figure. What can I glean from their narrative?
11. What or who do I fear? Why?
12. How does God want me to listen to him?
13. What is the "next step" for my spiritual growth?
14. Am I pleasing God in my singleness/ married life/ as a parent?
15. Is there anything in my life that I should put my trust in the Lord for?
16. Describe the three most vulnerable areas of myself.
17. Describe three occasions in my life when the Lord provided for me and served as my protection.
18. According to Ecclesiastes, there is a season for everything. Which season am I now in?
19. Write my own Psalm of praise/thanksgiving to God.
20. When did Jesus Christ become my Lord and Savior?
21. How might I live within the anointing of the Lord?
22. Recall a period in my life when the Lord delivered me.
23. In my perspective, what will heaven be like?
24. What might I do this year to improve my patience?
25. How could I become more grateful this year?
26. Is it possible that I'm growing arrogant in some way? How can I make it right?
27. How can I make this year more enjoyable?
28. How can I make this year a more peaceful one for myself?
29. What could I do this year to cultivate obedience to the Lord?
30. How can I love more this year?
31. How can I become nicer and gentler this year?
32. Write a letter of forgiveness to an enemy.
33. If I am struggling with something, what do I think God wants me to learn from it?
34. What spiritual gifts do I possess? What can I do with them to further God's kingdom?
35. Write on a time when the Lord spoke to me.
36. Be still and listen. What is the Lord revealing to me at this moment?
37. When do I most strongly feel God's presence? What can I do when I don't feel His presence near?
38. The last time something angered me, how did I react to it? What does the reply reveal about my character?
39. How does my pride respond when something offends me?
40. How can I experience the Lord's healing in my life?
41. Who is one individual I can specifically help? How?
42. What steals my peace by diverting my thoughts from God?
43. When have I sensed God's grasp and presence lifting me up?
44. What component of my relationship with the Lord makes me the most thankful?
45. Which Bible scripture is my favorite, and why?
46. Do I just celebrate when things are going well? Can I celebrate while in famine?
47. What transgressions must I repent of to the Lord?
48. Make a list of song lyrics that speak to me and explain why.
49. What has been the greatest blessing so far in my life?
50. What am I sensing God calling me to change in my life?

IT'S ALL ABOUT JESUS

Weekly Bible Goals/Faith In Action

Date: _____

Sunday	
Monday	
Tuesday	
Wednesday	
Thursday	
Friday	
Saturday	

IT'S ALL ABOUT JESUS

Weekly Reflection

Before I Start My Week:	After My Week Ends:
What am I grateful for?	How did I see God working in me?
What does God want me to do this week?	Was I honoring God with my actions?
What area do I want God to bless me?	What things could I have done differently?
How can I be Salt & Light to my community?	How did I reflect Christ's love this week?

IT'S ALL ABOUT JESUS

Scripture Studied

Author:_____ Where:_____

When:_____   Why:_____

Scripture:

Cross Reverences::

Observation:

Application:

Notes:

Summary of What I Learned

Important Locations:

Memory Verse

Key Words:

Key People:

Questions:

IT'S ALL ABOUT JESUS

Weekly Prayer

My Prayer Focus:

My praise and worship
_____
_____
_____
_____

Lord I am grateful for...
_____
_____
_____
_____

Lord teach me to....
_____
_____
_____
_____

What are the struggles I am facing?
_____
_____
_____
_____

What may be God's answer to my prayer?
_____
_____
_____
_____

Prayer:
_____
_____
_____
_____
_____
_____
_____
_____
_____
_____
_____
_____
_____
_____
_____
_____
_____
_____
_____
_____
_____
_____
_____
_____

Weekly Revelation

How did the Lord speak to me?

Discription of what I saw/heard:

How do I feel about this revelation?

What may be the interpretation?

Biblical References:

- _____
- _____
- _____
- _____
- _____

IT'S ALL ABOUT JESUS

Weekly Self-Reflection

Verse:_____   Topic:_____

What's the context?

_____
_____
_____

My initial thoughts:

_____
_____
_____

Similar Verses:

- _____
- _____
- _____
- _____
- _____
- _____

What immediately stands out to me about this verse?

_____
_____
_____
_____
_____

Does this show me how Christians are supposed to live?

_____
_____
_____
_____
_____

Is there an example of this verse in the first 5 books of the Bible?

_____
_____
_____
_____

Does this remind me of anything Jesus said or did?

_____
_____
_____
_____

IT'S ALL ABOUT JESUS

Weekly Self-Reflection

Question I am pondering about today:

IT'S ALL ABOUT JESUS

Self-Reflection Journal Prompts

1. What is God asking me to prioritize over the upcoming six months?
2. Today, God has given me someone to pray for.
3. Is my behavior this week indicating that I'm content with my life circumstances?
4. Who is God urging me to let go of my grudge against?
5. What aspects of the fruit of the Spirit do I need to enlist assistance in developing?
6. How can I help others by shining a light in a dark place?
7. Is there a time when I feel the most distant from the Lord?
8. How is my arrogance driving me to cause harm to others?
9. Do I find it difficult to communicate my regrets? If that's the case, why?
10. Choose a Biblical figure. What can I glean from their narrative?
11. What or who do I fear? Why?
12. How does God want me to listen to him?
13. What is the "next step" for my spiritual growth?
14. Am I pleasing God in my singleness/ married life/ as a parent?
15. Is there anything in my life that I should put my trust in the Lord for?
16. Describe the three most vulnerable areas of myself.
17. Describe three occasions in my life when the Lord provided for me and served as my protection.
18. According to Ecclesiastes, there is a season for everything. Which season am I now in?
19. Write my own Psalm of praise/thanksgiving to God.
20. When did Jesus Christ become my Lord and Savior?
21. How might I live within the anointing of the Lord?
22. Recall a period in my life when the Lord delivered me.
23. In my perspective, what will heaven be like?
24. What might I do this year to improve my patience?
25. How could I become more grateful this year?
26. Is it possible that I'm growing arrogant in some way? How can I make it right?
27. How can I make this year more enjoyable?
28. How can I make this year a more peaceful one for myself?
29. What could I do this year to cultivate obedience to the Lord?
30. How can I love more this year?
31. How can I become nicer and gentler this year?
32. Write a letter of forgiveness to an enemy.
33. If I am struggling with something, what do I think God wants me to learn from it?
34. What spiritual gifts do I possess? What can I do with them to further God's kingdom?
35. Write on a time when the Lord spoke to me.
36. Be still and listen. What is the Lord revealing to me at this moment?
37. When do I most strongly feel God's presence? What can I do when I don't feel His presence near?
38. The last time something angered me, how did I react to it? What does the reply reveal about my character?
39. How does my pride respond when something offends me?
40. How can I experience the Lord's healing in my life?
41. Who is one individual I can specifically help? How?
42. What steals my peace by diverting my thoughts from God?
43. When have I sensed God's grasp and presence lifting me up?
44. What component of my relationship with the Lord makes me the most thankful?
45. Which Bible scripture is my favorite, and why?
46. Do I just celebrate when things are going well? Can I celebrate while in famine?
47. What transgressions must I repent of to the Lord?
48. Make a list of song lyrics that speak to me and explain why.
49. What has been the greatest blessing so far in my life?
50. What am I sensing God calling me to change in my life?

IT'S ALL ABOUT JESUS

April

"Looking for a word from the Lord? Believe that he has already spoken, and read what he's already written."
—Mark Driscoll

April

1. ___
2. ___
3. ___
4. ___
5. ___
6. ___
7. ___
8. ___
9. ___
10. ___
11. ___
12. ___
13. ___
14. ___
15. ___
16. ___
17. ___
18. ___
19. ___
20. ___
21. ___
22. ___
23. ___
24. ___
25. ___
26. ___
27. ___
28. ___
29. ___
30. ___

Monthly Intention	Monthly Reflection
This month's prayer focus:	What I'm thankful for this month:
To make this month great I will:	What I have learned about God:
What I'm looking forward to this month:	Who I served this month:

Weekly Bible Goals/Faith In Action

Date: _____

Sunday	
Monday	
Tuesday	
Wednesday	
Thursday	
Friday	
Saturday	

IT'S ALL ABOUT JESUS

Weekly Reflection

Before I Start My Week:

What am I grateful for?

What does God want me to do this week?

What area do I want God to bless me?

How can I be Salt & Light to my community?

After My Week Ends:

How did I see God working in me?

Was I honoring God with my actions?

What things could I have done differently?

How did I reflect Christ's love this week?

Scripture Studied

Author:_____ Where:_____

When:_____ Why:_____

Scripture:

Cross Reverences::

Observation:

Application:

Notes:
_____
_____
_____
_____
_____
_____

IT'S ALL ABOUT JESUS

Summary of What I Learned

Important Locations:

Memory Verse

Key Words:

Questions:

Key People:

IT'S ALL ABOUT JESUS

Weekly Prayer

My Prayer Focus:

My praise and worship

_____
_____
_____

Lord I am grateful for...

_____
_____
_____

Lord teach me to....

_____
_____
_____

What are the struggles I am facing?

_____
_____
_____

What may be God's answer to my prayer?

_____
_____
_____

Prayer:

_____
_____
_____
_____
_____
_____
_____
_____
_____
_____
_____
_____
_____
_____
_____
_____
_____
_____
_____
_____

IT'S ALL ABOUT JESUS

Weekly Revelation

How did the Lord speak to me?
_____
_____
_____
_____
_____

Discription of what I saw/heard:

How do I feel about this revelation?
_____
_____
_____
_____
_____
_____

What may be the interpretation?
_____
_____
_____
_____
_____
_____
_____
_____
_____
_____
_____

Biblical References:
- _____
- _____
- _____
- _____
- _____

It's All About Jesus

Weekly Self-Reflection

Verse:_____   Topic:_____

What's the context?

_____
_____
_____

My initial thoughts:

_____
_____
_____

Similar Verses:

- _____
- _____
- _____
- _____
- _____
- _____

What immediately stands out to me about this verse?

_____
_____
_____
_____

Does this show me how Christians are supposed to live?

_____
_____
_____
_____

Is there an example of this verse in the first 5 books of the Bible?

_____
_____
_____
_____

Does this remind me of anything Jesus said or did?

_____
_____
_____
_____

IT'S ALL ABOUT JESUS

Weekly Self-Reflection

Question I am pondering about today:

Self-Reflection Journal Prompts

1. What is God asking me to prioritize over the upcoming six months?
2. Today, God has given me someone to pray for.
3. Is my behavior this week indicating that I'm content with my life circumstances?
4. Who is God urging me to let go of my grudge against?
5. What aspects of the fruit of the Spirit do I need to enlist assistance in developing?
6. How can I help others by shining a light in a dark place?
7. Is there a time when I feel the most distant from the Lord?
8. How is my arrogance driving me to cause harm to others?
9. Do I find it difficult to communicate my regrets? If that's the case, why?
10. Choose a Biblical figure. What can I glean from their narrative?
11. What or who do I fear? Why?
12. How does God want me to listen to him?
13. What is the "next step" for my spiritual growth?
14. Am I pleasing God in my singleness/ married life/ as a parent?
15. Is there anything in my life that I should put my trust in the Lord for?
16. Describe the three most vulnerable areas of myself.
17. Describe three occasions in my life when the Lord provided for me and served as my protection.
18. According to Ecclesiastes, there is a season for everything. Which season am I now in?
19. Write my own Psalm of praise/thanksgiving to God.
20. When did Jesus Christ become my Lord and Savior?
21. How might I live within the anointing of the Lord?
22. Recall a period in my life when the Lord delivered me.
23. In my perspective, what will heaven be like?
24. What might I do this year to improve my patience?
25. How could I become more grateful this year?
26. Is it possible that I'm growing arrogant in some way? How can I make it right?
27. How can I make this year more enjoyable?
28. How can I make this year a more peaceful one for myself?
29. What could I do this year to cultivate obedience to the Lord?
30. How can I love more this year?
31. How can I become nicer and gentler this year?
32. Write a letter of forgiveness to an enemy.
33. If I am struggling with something, what do I think God wants me to learn from it?
34. What spiritual gifts do I possess? What can I do with them to further God's kingdom?
35. Write on a time when the Lord spoke to me.
36. Be still and listen. What is the Lord revealing to me at this moment?
37. When do I most strongly feel God's presence? What can I do when I don't feel His presence near?
38. The last time something angered me, how did I react to it? What does the reply reveal about my character?
39. How does my pride respond when something offends me?
40. How can I experience the Lord's healing in my life?
41. Who is one individual I can specifically help? How?
42. What steals my peace by diverting my thoughts from God?
43. When have I sensed God's grasp and presence lifting me up?
44. What component of my relationship with the Lord makes me the most thankful?
45. Which Bible scripture is my favorite, and why?
46. Do I just celebrate when things are going well? Can I celebrate while in famine?
47. What transgressions must I repent of to the Lord?
48. Make a list of song lyrics that speak to me and explain why.
49. What has been the greatest blessing so far in my life?
50. What am I sensing God calling me to change in my life?

IT'S ALL ABOUT JESUS

Weekly Bible Goals/Faith In Action

Date: _____

Sunday	
Monday	
Tuesday	
Wednesday	
Thursday	
Friday	
Saturday	

Weekly Reflection

Before I Start My Week:

What am I grateful for?

What does God want me to do this week?

What area do I want God to bless me?

How can I be Salt & Light to my community?

After My Week Ends:

How did I see God working in me?

Was I honoring God with my actions?

What things could I have done differently?

How did I reflect Christ's love this week?

IT'S ALL ABOUT JESUS

Scripture Studied

Author:_____   Where:_____

When:_____   Why:_____

Scripture:

Cross Reverences::

Observation:

Application:

Notes:

Summary of What I Learned

Important Locations:

Memory Verse

Key Words:

Questions:

Key People:

IT'S ALL ABOUT JESUS

Weekly Prayer

My Prayer focus:

My praise and worship

Lord I am grateful for...

Lord teach me to....

What are the struggles I am facing?

What may be God's answer to my prayer?

Prayer:

Weekly Revelation

How did the Lord speak to me?
_____
_____
_____
_____
_____

Discription of what I saw/heard:

How do I feel about this revelation?
_____
_____
_____
_____
_____
_____

What may be the interpretation?
_____
_____
_____
_____
_____
_____
_____
_____
_____
_____

Biblical References:
- _____
- _____
- _____
- _____
- _____

IT'S ALL ABOUT JESUS

Weekly Self-Reflection

Verse:_____   Topic:_____

What's the context?
_____
_____
_____

Similar Verses :
- _____
- _____
- _____
- _____
- _____
- _____

My initial thoughts:
_____
_____
_____

What immediately stands out to me about this verse?
_____
_____
_____
_____
_____

Does this show me how Christians are supposed to live?
_____
_____
_____
_____
_____

Is there an example of this verse in the first 5 books of the Bible?
_____
_____
_____
_____

Does this remind me of anything Jesus said or did?
_____
_____
_____
_____
_____

Weekly Self-Reflection

Question I am pondering about today:

IT'S ALL ABOUT JESUS

Self-Reflection Journal Prompts

1. What is God asking me to prioritize over the upcoming six months?
2. Today, God has given me someone to pray for.
3. Is my behavior this week indicating that I'm content with my life circumstances?
4. Who is God urging me to let go of my grudge against?
5. What aspects of the fruit of the Spirit do I need to enlist assistance in developing?
6. How can I help others by shining a light in a dark place?
7. Is there a time when I feel the most distant from the Lord?
8. How is my arrogance driving me to cause harm to others?
9. Do I find it difficult to communicate my regrets? If that's the case, why?
10. Choose a Biblical figure. What can I glean from their narrative?
11. What or who do I fear? Why?
12. How does God want me to listen to him?
13. What is the "next step" for my spiritual growth?
14. Am I pleasing God in my singleness/ married life/ as a parent?
15. Is there anything in my life that I should put my trust in the Lord for?
16. Describe the three most vulnerable areas of myself.
17. Describe three occasions in my life when the Lord provided for me and served as my protection.
18. According to Ecclesiastes, there is a season for everything. Which season am I now in?
19. Write my own Psalm of praise/thanksgiving to God.
20. When did Jesus Christ become my Lord and Savior?
21. How might I live within the anointing of the Lord?
22. Recall a period in my life when the Lord delivered me.
23. In my perspective, what will heaven be like?
24. What might I do this year to improve my patience?
25. How could I become more grateful this year?
26. Is it possible that I'm growing arrogant in some way? How can I make it right?
27. How can I make this year more enjoyable?
28. How can I make this year a more peaceful one for myself?
29. What could I do this year to cultivate obedience to the Lord?
30. How can I love more this year?
31. How can I become nicer and gentler this year?
32. Write a letter of forgiveness to an enemy.
33. If I am struggling with something, what do I think God wants me to learn from it?
34. What spiritual gifts do I possess? What can I do with them to further God's kingdom?
35. Write on a time when the Lord spoke to me.
36. Be still and listen. What is the Lord revealing to me at this moment?
37. When do I most strongly feel God's presence? What can I do when I don't feel His presence near?
38. The last time something angered me, how did I react to it? What does the reply reveal about my character?
39. How does my pride respond when something offends me?
40. How can I experience the Lord's healing in my life?
41. Who is one individual I can specifically help? How?
42. What steals my peace by diverting my thoughts from God?
43. When have I sensed God's grasp and presence lifting me up?
44. What component of my relationship with the Lord makes me the most thankful?
45. Which Bible scripture is my favorite, and why?
46. Do I just celebrate when things are going well? Can I celebrate while in famine?
47. What transgressions must I repent of to the Lord?
48. Make a list of song lyrics that speak to me and explain why.
49. What has been the greatest blessing so far in my life?
50. What am I sensing God calling me to change in my life?

IT'S ALL ABOUT JESUS

Weekly Bible Goals/Faith In Action

Date: _____

Sunday	
Monday	
Tuesday	
Wednesday	
Thursday	
Friday	
Saturday	

IT'S ALL ABOUT JESUS

Weekly Reflection

Before I Start My Week:

What am I grateful for?

What does God want me to do this week?

What area do I want God to bless me?

How can I be Salt & Light to my community?

After My Week Ends:

How did I see God working in me?

Was I honoring God with my actions?

What things could I have done differently?

How did I reflect Christ's love this week?

Scripture Studied

Author:_____ Where:_____

When:_____ Why:_____

Scripture:

Cross Reverences::

Observation:

Application:

Notes:

IT'S ALL ABOUT JESUS

Summary of What I Learned

Important Locations:

Memory Verse

Key Words:

Questions:

Key People:

Weekly Prayer

My Prayer Focus:

My praise and worship

Lord I am grateful for...

Lord teach me to....

What are the struggles I am facing?

What may be God's answer to my prayer?

Prayer:

IT'S ALL ABOUT JESUS

Weekly Revelation

How did the Lord speak to me?
_____
_____
_____
_____

Discription of what I saw/heard:

How do I feel about this revelation?
_____
_____
_____
_____
_____

What may be the interpretation?
_____
_____
_____
_____
_____
_____
_____
_____

Biblical References :
- _____
- _____
- _____
- _____
- _____

Weekly Self-Reflection

Verse:_____   Topic:_____

What's the context?

_____
_____
_____

My initial thoughts:

_____
_____
_____
_____

Similar Verses :
- _____
- _____
- _____
- _____
- _____
- _____

What immediately stands out to me about this verse?

_____
_____
_____
_____

Does this show me how Christians are supposed to live?

_____
_____
_____
_____

Is there an example of this verse in the first 5 books of the Bible?

_____
_____
_____
_____

Does this remind me of anything Jesus said or did?

_____
_____
_____
_____

IT'S ALL ABOUT JESUS

Weekly Self-Reflection

Question I am pondering about today:

Self-Reflection Journal Prompts

1. What is God asking me to prioritize over the upcoming six months?
2. Today, God has given me someone to pray for.
3. Is my behavior this week indicating that I'm content with my life circumstances?
4. Who is God urging me to let go of my grudge against?
5. What aspects of the fruit of the Spirit do I need to enlist assistance in developing?
6. How can I help others by shining a light in a dark place?
7. Is there a time when I feel the most distant from the Lord?
8. How is my arrogance driving me to cause harm to others?
9. Do I find it difficult to communicate my regrets? If that's the case, why?
10. Choose a Biblical figure. What can I glean from their narrative?
11. What or who do I fear? Why?
12. How does God want me to listen to him?
13. What is the "next step" for my spiritual growth?
14. Am I pleasing God in my singleness/ married life/ as a parent?
15. Is there anything in my life that I should put my trust in the Lord for?
16. Describe the three most vulnerable areas of myself.
17. Describe three occasions in my life when the Lord provided for me and served as my protection.
18. According to Ecclesiastes, there is a season for everything. Which season am I now in?
19. Write my own Psalm of praise/thanksgiving to God.
20. When did Jesus Christ become my Lord and Savior?
21. How might I live within the anointing of the Lord?
22. Recall a period in my life when the Lord delivered me.
23. In my perspective, what will heaven be like?
24. What might I do this year to improve my patience?
25. How could I become more grateful this year?
26. Is it possible that I'm growing arrogant in some way? How can I make it right?
27. How can I make this year more enjoyable?
28. How can I make this year a more peaceful one for myself?
29. What could I do this year to cultivate obedience to the Lord?
30. How can I love more this year?
31. How can I become nicer and gentler this year?
32. Write a letter of forgiveness to an enemy.
33. If I am struggling with something, what do I think God wants me to learn from it?
34. What spiritual gifts do I possess? What can I do with them to further God's kingdom?
35. Write on a time when the Lord spoke to me.
36. Be still and listen. What is the Lord revealing to me at this moment?
37. When do I most strongly feel God's presence? What can I do when I don't feel His presence near?
38. The last time something angered me, how did I react to it? What does the reply reveal about my character?
39. How does my pride respond when something offends me?
40. How can I experience the Lord's healing in my life?
41. Who is one individual I can specifically help? How?
42. What steals my peace by diverting my thoughts from God?
43. When have I sensed God's grasp and presence lifting me up?
44. What component of my relationship with the Lord makes me the most thankful?
45. Which Bible scripture is my favorite, and why?
46. Do I just celebrate when things are going well? Can I celebrate while in famine?
47. What transgressions must I repent of to the Lord?
48. Make a list of song lyrics that speak to me and explain why.
49. What has been the greatest blessing so far in my life?
50. What am I sensing God calling me to change in my life?

IT'S ALL ABOUT JESUS

Weekly Bible Goals/Faith In Action

Date: _____

Sunday	
Monday	
Tuesday	
Wednesday	
Thursday	
Friday	
Saturday	

Weekly Reflection

Before I Start My Week:

What am I grateful for?

What does God want me to do this week?

What area do I want God to bless me?

How can I be Salt & Light to my community?

After My Week Ends:

How did I see God working in me?

Was I honoring God with my actions?

What things could I have done differently?

How did I reflect Christ's love this week?

IT'S ALL ABOUT JESUS

Scripture Studied

Author:_____ Where:_____

When:_____ Why:_____

Scripture:

Cross Reverences::

Observation:

Application:

Notes:

Summary of What I Learned

Important Locations:

Memory Verse

Key Words:

Questions:

Key People:

IT'S ALL ABOUT JESUS

Weekly Prayer

My Prayer Focus:

My praise and worship

_____
_____
_____
_____

Lord I am grateful for...

_____
_____
_____
_____

Lord teach me to....

_____
_____
_____
_____

What are the struggles I am facing?

_____
_____
_____
_____

What may be God's answer to my prayer?

_____
_____
_____
_____

Prayer:

_____
_____
_____
_____
_____
_____
_____
_____
_____
_____
_____
_____
_____
_____
_____
_____
_____
_____
_____
_____
_____
_____
_____
_____
_____
_____

Weekly Revelation

How did the Lord speak to me?
_____
_____
_____
_____
_____

Discription of what I saw/heard:

How do I feel about this revelation?
_____
_____
_____
_____
_____
_____

What may be the interpretation?
_____
_____
_____
_____
_____
_____
_____
_____
_____
_____

Biblical References:
- _____
- _____
- _____
- _____
- _____

IT'S ALL ABOUT JESUS

Weekly Self-Reflection

Verse:_____ Topic:_____

What's the context?
_____
_____
_____

My initial thoughts:
_____
_____
_____

Similar Verses:
- _____
- _____
- _____
- _____
- _____
- _____

What immediately stands out to me about this verse?
_____
_____
_____
_____

Does this show me how Christians are supposed to live?
_____
_____
_____
_____

Is there an example of this verse in the first 5 books of the Bible?
_____
_____
_____
_____

Does this remind me of anything Jesus said or did?
_____
_____
_____
_____

Weekly Self-Reflection

Question I am pondering about today:

IT'S ALL ABOUT JESUS

Self-Reflection Journal Prompts

1. What is God asking me to prioritize over the upcoming six months?
2. Today, God has given me someone to pray for.
3. Is my behavior this week indicating that I'm content with my life circumstances?
4. Who is God urging me to let go of my grudge against?
5. What aspects of the fruit of the Spirit do I need to enlist assistance in developing?
6. How can I help others by shining a light in a dark place?
7. Is there a time when I feel the most distant from the Lord?
8. How is my arrogance driving me to cause harm to others?
9. Do I find it difficult to communicate my regrets? If that's the case, why?
10. Choose a Biblical figure. What can I glean from their narrative?
11. What or who do I fear? Why?
12. How does God want me to listen to him?
13. What is the "next step" for my spiritual growth?
14. Am I pleasing God in my singleness/ married life/ as a parent?
15. Is there anything in my life that I should put my trust in the Lord for?
16. Describe the three most vulnerable areas of myself.
17. Describe three occasions in my life when the Lord provided for me and served as my protection.
18. According to Ecclesiastes, there is a season for everything. Which season am I now in?
19. Write my own Psalm of praise/thanksgiving to God.
20. When did Jesus Christ become my Lord and Savior?
21. How might I live within the anointing of the Lord?
22. Recall a period in my life when the Lord delivered me.
23. In my perspective, what will heaven be like?
24. What might I do this year to improve my patience?
25. How could I become more grateful this year?
26. Is it possible that I'm growing arrogant in some way? How can I make it right?
27. How can I make this year more enjoyable?
28. How can I make this year a more peaceful one for myself?
29. What could I do this year to cultivate obedience to the Lord?
30. How can I love more this year?
31. How can I become nicer and gentler this year?
32. Write a letter of forgiveness to an enemy.
33. If I am struggling with something, what do I think God wants me to learn from it?
34. What spiritual gifts do I possess? What can I do with them to further God's kingdom?
35. Write on a time when the Lord spoke to me.
36. Be still and listen. What is the Lord revealing to me at this moment?
37. When do I most strongly feel God's presence? What can I do when I don't feel His presence near?
38. The last time something angered me, how did I react to it? What does the reply reveal about my character?
39. How does my pride respond when something offends me?
40. How can I experience the Lord's healing in my life?
41. Who is one individual I can specifically help? How?
42. What steals my peace by diverting my thoughts from God?
43. When have I sensed God's grasp and presence lifting me up?
44. What component of my relationship with the Lord makes me the most thankful?
45. Which Bible scripture is my favorite, and why?
46. Do I just celebrate when things are going well? Can I celebrate while in famine?
47. What transgressions must I repent of to the Lord?
48. Make a list of song lyrics that speak to me and explain why.
49. What has been the greatest blessing so far in my life?
50. What am I sensing God calling me to change in my life?

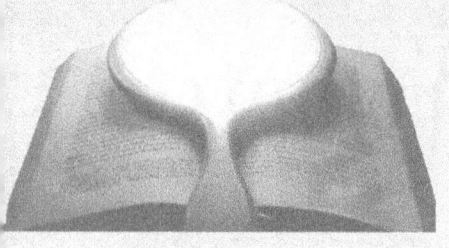

May

"The Bible must not be read as a job description for motivated, self-disciplined, devoutly religious people to be their own heroes and saviors of their souls. It must be read as the story of guilty sinners and self-righteous hypocrites, visited by a perfect God"
—Mark Driscoll

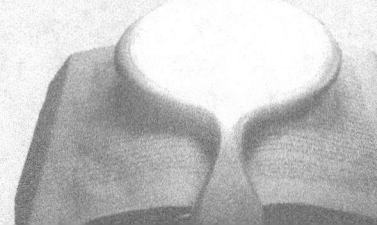

May

1. _____
2. _____
3. _____
4. _____
5. _____
6. _____
7. _____
8. _____
9. _____
10. _____
11. _____
12. _____
13. _____
14. _____
15. _____
16. _____
17. _____
18. _____
19. _____
20. _____
21. _____
22. _____
23. _____
24. _____
25. _____
26. _____
27. _____
28. _____
29. _____
30. _____
31. _____

Monthly Intention	Monthly Reflection
This month's prayer focus:	What I'm thankful for this month:
To make this month great I will:	What I have learned about God:
What I'm looking forward to this month:	Who I served this month:

Weekly Bible Goals/Faith In Action

Date: _____

Sunday	
Monday	
Tuesday	
Wednesday	
Thursday	
Friday	
Saturday	

IT'S ALL ABOUT JESUS

Weekly Reflection

Before I Start My Week:	After My Week Ends:
What am I grateful for?	How did I see God working in me?
What does God want me to do this week?	Was I honoring God with my actions?
What area do I want God to bless me?	What things could I have done differently?
How can I be Salt & Light to my community?	How did I reflect Christ's love this week?

Scripture Studied

Author:_____ Where:_____

When:_____ Why:_____

Scripture:

Cross Reverences::
_____
_____
_____
_____

Observation:

Application:

Notes:
_____
_____
_____
_____
_____
_____
_____

IT'S ALL ABOUT JESUS

Summary of What I Learned

Important Locations:

Memory Verse

Key Words:

Key People:

Questions:

IT'S ALL ABOUT JESUS

Weekly Prayer

My Prayer Focus:

My praise and worship

_____
_____
_____

Lord I am grateful for...

_____
_____
_____

Lord teach me to....

_____
_____
_____

What are the struggles I am facing?

_____
_____
_____

What may be God's answer to my prayer?

_____
_____
_____

Prayer:

_____
_____
_____
_____
_____
_____
_____
_____
_____
_____
_____
_____
_____
_____
_____
_____
_____
_____
_____
_____

IT'S ALL ABOUT JESUS

Weekly Revelation

How did the Lord speak to me?

_____
_____
_____
_____

Discription of what I saw/heard:

How do I feel about this revelation?

_____
_____
_____
_____

What may be the interpretation?

_____
_____
_____
_____
_____
_____
_____
_____

Biblical References:

- _____
- _____
- _____
- _____
- _____

IT'S ALL ABOUT JESUS

Weekly Self-Reflection

Verse:_____   Topic:_____

What's the context?
_____
_____
_____

My initial thoughts:
_____
_____
_____
_____

Similar Verses:
- _____
- _____
- _____
- _____
- _____
- _____

What immediately stands out to me about this verse?
_____
_____
_____
_____

Does this show me how Christians are supposed to live?
_____
_____
_____
_____
_____

Is there an example of this verse in the first 5 books of the Bible?
_____
_____
_____
_____

Does this remind me of anything Jesus said or did?
_____
_____
_____
_____

IT'S ALL ABOUT JESUS

Weekly Self-Reflection

Question I am pondering about today:

Self-Reflection Journal Prompts

1. What is God asking me to prioritize over the upcoming six months?
2. Today, God has given me someone to pray for.
3. Is my behavior this week indicating that I'm content with my life circumstances?
4. Who is God urging me to let go of my grudge against?
5. What aspects of the fruit of the Spirit do I need to enlist assistance in developing?
6. How can I help others by shining a light in a dark place?
7. Is there a time when I feel the most distant from the Lord?
8. How is my arrogance driving me to cause harm to others?
9. Do I find it difficult to communicate my regrets? If that's the case, why?
10. Choose a Biblical figure. What can I glean from their narrative?
11. What or who do I fear? Why?
12. How does God want me to listen to him?
13. What is the "next step" for my spiritual growth?
14. Am I pleasing God in my singleness/ married life/ as a parent?
15. Is there anything in my life that I should put my trust in the Lord for?
16. Describe the three most vulnerable areas of myself.
17. Describe three occasions in my life when the Lord provided for me and served as my protection.
18. According to Ecclesiastes, there is a season for everything. Which season am I now in?
19. Write my own Psalm of praise/thanksgiving to God.
20. When did Jesus Christ become my Lord and Savior?
21. How might I live within the anointing of the Lord?
22. Recall a period in my life when the Lord delivered me.
23. In my perspective, what will heaven be like?
24. What might I do this year to improve my patience?
25. How could I become more grateful this year?
26. Is it possible that I'm growing arrogant in some way? How can I make it right?
27. How can I make this year more enjoyable?
28. How can I make this year a more peaceful one for myself?
29. What could I do this year to cultivate obedience to the Lord?
30. How can I love more this year?
31. How can I become nicer and gentler this year?
32. Write a letter of forgiveness to an enemy.
33. If I am struggling with something, what do I think God wants me to learn from it?
34. What spiritual gifts do I possess? What can I do with them to further God's kingdom?
35. Write on a time when the Lord spoke to me.
36. Be still and listen. What is the Lord revealing to me at this moment?
37. When do I most strongly feel God's presence? What can I do when I don't feel His presence near?
38. The last time something angered me, how did I react to it? What does the reply reveal about my character?
39. How does my pride respond when something offends me?
40. How can I experience the Lord's healing in my life?
41. Who is one individual I can specifically help? How?
42. What steals my peace by diverting my thoughts from God?
43. When have I sensed God's grasp and presence lifting me up?
44. What component of my relationship with the Lord makes me the most thankful?
45. Which Bible scripture is my favorite, and why?
46. Do I just celebrate when things are going well? Can I celebrate while in famine?
47. What transgressions must I repent of to the Lord?
48. Make a list of song lyrics that speak to me and explain why.
49. What has been the greatest blessing so far in my life?
50. What am I sensing God calling me to change in my life?

IT'S ALL ABOUT JESUS

Weekly Bible Goals/Faith In Action

Date: _____

Sunday	
Monday	
Tuesday	
Wednesday	
Thursday	
Friday	
Saturday	

IT'S ALL ABOUT JESUS

Weekly Reflection

Before I Start My Week:	After My Week Ends:
What am I grateful for?	How did I see God working in me?
What does God want me to do this week?	Was I honoring God with my actions?
What area do I want God to bless me?	What things could I have done differently?
How can I be Salt & Light to my community?	How did I reflect Christ's love this week?

IT'S ALL ABOUT JESUS

Scripture Studied

Author:_____   Where:_____

When:_____   Why:_____

Scripture:

Cross Reverences::

Observation:

Application:

Notes:

Summary of What I Learned

Important Locations:

Memory Verse

Key Words:
-
-
-
-
-

Questions:
-
-
-
-

Key People:
-
-
-
-

IT'S ALL ABOUT JESUS

Weekly Prayer

My Prayer Focus:

My praise and worship

Lord I am grateful for...

Lord teach me to....

What are the struggles I am facing?

What may be God's answer to my prayer?

Prayer:

IT'S ALL ABOUT JESUS

Weekly Revelation

How did the Lord speak to me?

Discription of what I saw/heard:

How do I feel about this revelation?

What may be the interpretation?

Biblical References:
- _____
- _____
- _____
- _____
- _____

IT'S ALL ABOUT JESUS

Weekly Self-Reflection

Verse:_____   Topic:_____

What's the context?

_____
_____
_____

My initial thoughts:

_____
_____
_____

Similar Verses:

- _____
- _____
- _____
- _____
- _____
- _____

What immediately stands out to me about this verse?

_____
_____
_____
_____

Does this show me how Christians are supposed to live?

_____
_____
_____
_____

Is there an example of this verse in the first 5 books of the Bible?

_____
_____
_____
_____

Does this remind me of anything Jesus said or did?

_____
_____
_____
_____

IT'S ALL ABOUT JESUS

Weekly Self-Reflection

Question I am pondering about today:

IT'S ALL ABOUT JESUS

Self-Reflection Journal Prompts

1. What is God asking me to prioritize over the upcoming six months?
2. Today, God has given me someone to pray for.
3. Is my behavior this week indicating that I'm content with my life circumstances?
4. Who is God urging me to let go of my grudge against?
5. What aspects of the fruit of the Spirit do I need to enlist assistance in developing?
6. How can I help others by shining a light in a dark place?
7. Is there a time when I feel the most distant from the Lord?
8. How is my arrogance driving me to cause harm to others?
9. Do I find it difficult to communicate my regrets? If that's the case, why?
10. Choose a Biblical figure. What can I glean from their narrative?
11. What or who do I fear? Why?
12. How does God want me to listen to him?
13. What is the "next step" for my spiritual growth?
14. Am I pleasing God in my singleness/ married life/ as a parent?
15. Is there anything in my life that I should put my trust in the Lord for?
16. Describe the three most vulnerable areas of myself.
17. Describe three occasions in my life when the Lord provided for me and served as my protection.
18. According to Ecclesiastes, there is a season for everything. Which season am I now in?
19. Write my own Psalm of praise/thanksgiving to God.
20. When did Jesus Christ become my Lord and Savior?
21. How might I live within the anointing of the Lord?
22. Recall a period in my life when the Lord delivered me.
23. In my perspective, what will heaven be like?
24. What might I do this year to improve my patience?
25. How could I become more grateful this year?
26. Is it possible that I'm growing arrogant in some way? How can I make it right?
27. How can I make this year more enjoyable?
28. How can I make this year a more peaceful one for myself?
29. What could I do this year to cultivate obedience to the Lord?
30. How can I love more this year?
31. How can I become nicer and gentler this year?
32. Write a letter of forgiveness to an enemy.
33. If I am struggling with something, what do I think God wants me to learn from it?
34. What spiritual gifts do I possess? What can I do with them to further God's kingdom?
35. Write on a time when the Lord spoke to me.
36. Be still and listen. What is the Lord revealing to me at this moment?
37. When do I most strongly feel God's presence? What can I do when I don't feel His presence near?
38. The last time something angered me, how did I react to it? What does the reply reveal about my character?
39. How does my pride respond when something offends me?
40. How can I experience the Lord's healing in my life?
41. Who is one individual I can specifically help? How?
42. What steals my peace by diverting my thoughts from God?
43. When have I sensed God's grasp and presence lifting me up?
44. What component of my relationship with the Lord makes me the most thankful?
45. Which Bible scripture is my favorite, and why?
46. Do I just celebrate when things are going well? Can I celebrate while in famine?
47. What transgressions must I repent of to the Lord?
48. Make a list of song lyrics that speak to me and explain why.
49. What has been the greatest blessing so far in my life?
50. What am I sensing God calling me to change in my life?

Weekly Bible Goals/Faith In Action

Date: _____

Sunday	
Monday	
Tuesday	
Wednesday	
Thursday	
Friday	
Saturday	

IT'S ALL ABOUT JESUS

Weekly Reflection

Before I Start My Week:

What am I grateful for?

What does God want me to do this week?

What area do I want God to bless me?

How can I be Salt & Light to my community?

After My Week Ends:

How did I see God working in me?

Was I honoring God with my actions?

What things could I have done differently?

How did I reflect Christ's love this week?

Scripture Studied

Author:_____   Where:_____

When:_____   Why:_____

Scripture:

Cross Reverences::

Observation:

Application:

Notes:

IT'S ALL ABOUT JESUS

Summary of What I Learned

Important Locations:

Memory Verse

Key Words:

Questions:

Key People:

IT'S ALL ABOUT JESUS

Weekly Prayer

My Prayer Focus:

My praise and worship

_____
_____
_____

Lord I am grateful for...

_____
_____
_____
_____

Lord teach me to....

_____
_____
_____
_____

What are the struggles I am facing?

_____
_____
_____
_____

What may be God's answer to my prayer?

_____
_____
_____

Prayer:

_____
_____
_____
_____
_____
_____
_____
_____
_____
_____
_____
_____
_____
_____
_____
_____
_____
_____
_____
_____
_____
_____
_____
_____
_____
_____
_____
_____

IT'S ALL ABOUT JESUS

Weekly Revelation

How did the Lord speak to me?
_____
_____
_____
_____

Discription of what I saw/heard:

How do I feel about this revelation?
_____
_____
_____
_____
_____

What may be the interpretation?
_____
_____
_____
_____
_____
_____
_____
_____
_____

Biblical References:
- _____
- _____
- _____
- _____
- _____

IT'S ALL ABOUT JESUS

Weekly Self-Reflection

Verse:_____ Topic:_____

What's the context?
_____
_____
_____

Similar Verses:
- _____
- _____
- _____
- _____
- _____
- _____

My initial thoughts:
_____
_____
_____

What immediately stands out to me about this verse?
_____
_____
_____
_____

Does this show me how Christians are supposed to live?
_____
_____
_____
_____

Is there an example of this verse in the first 5 books of the Bible?
_____
_____
_____
_____

Does this remind me of anything Jesus said or did?
_____
_____
_____
_____

IT'S ALL ABOUT JESUS

Weekly Self-Reflection

Question I am pondering about today:

Self-Reflection Journal Prompts

1. What is God asking me to prioritize over the upcoming six months?
2. Today, God has given me someone to pray for.
3. Is my behavior this week indicating that I'm content with my life circumstances?
4. Who is God urging me to let go of my grudge against?
5. What aspects of the fruit of the Spirit do I need to enlist assistance in developing?
6. How can I help others by shining a light in a dark place?
7. Is there a time when I feel the most distant from the Lord?
8. How is my arrogance driving me to cause harm to others?
9. Do I find it difficult to communicate my regrets? If that's the case, why?
10. Choose a Biblical figure. What can I glean from their narrative?
11. What or who do I fear? Why?
12. How does God want me to listen to him?
13. What is the "next step" for my spiritual growth?
14. Am I pleasing God in my singleness/ married life/ as a parent?
15. Is there anything in my life that I should put my trust in the Lord for?
16. Describe the three most vulnerable areas of myself.
17. Describe three occasions in my life when the Lord provided for me and served as my protection.
18. According to Ecclesiastes, there is a season for everything. Which season am I now in?
19. Write my own Psalm of praise/thanksgiving to God.
20. When did Jesus Christ become my Lord and Savior?
21. How might I live within the anointing of the Lord?
22. Recall a period in my life when the Lord delivered me.
23. In my perspective, what will heaven be like?
24. What might I do this year to improve my patience?
25. How could I become more grateful this year?
26. Is it possible that I'm growing arrogant in some way? How can I make it right?
27. How can I make this year more enjoyable?
28. How can I make this year a more peaceful one for myself?
29. What could I do this year to cultivate obedience to the Lord?
30. How can I love more this year?
31. How can I become nicer and gentler this year?
32. Write a letter of forgiveness to an enemy.
33. If I am struggling with something, what do I think God wants me to learn from it?
34. What spiritual gifts do I possess? What can I do with them to further God's kingdom?
35. Write on a time when the Lord spoke to me.
36. Be still and listen. What is the Lord revealing to me at this moment?
37. When do I most strongly feel God's presence? What can I do when I don't feel His presence near?
38. The last time something angered me, how did I react to it? What does the reply reveal about my character?
39. How does my pride respond when something offends me?
40. How can I experience the Lord's healing in my life?
41. Who is one individual I can specifically help? How?
42. What steals my peace by diverting my thoughts from God?
43. When have I sensed God's grasp and presence lifting me up?
44. What component of my relationship with the Lord makes me the most thankful?
45. Which Bible scripture is my favorite, and why?
46. Do I just celebrate when things are going well? Can I celebrate while in famine?
47. What transgressions must I repent of to the Lord?
48. Make a list of song lyrics that speak to me and explain why.
49. What has been the greatest blessing so far in my life?
50. What am I sensing God calling me to change in my life?

IT'S ALL ABOUT JESUS

Weekly Bible Goals/Faith In Action

Date: _____

Day	
Sunday	
Monday	
Tuesday	
Wednesday	
Thursday	
Friday	
Saturday	

Weekly Reflection

Before I Start My Week:

What am I grateful for?

What does God want me to do this week?

What area do I want God to bless me?

How can I be Salt & Light to my community?

After My Week Ends:

How did I see God working in me?

Was I honoring God with my actions?

What things could I have done differently?

How did I reflect Christ's love this week?

IT'S ALL ABOUT JESUS

Scripture Studied

Author:_____   Where:_____

When:_____   Why:_____

Scripture:

Cross Reverences::

Observation:

Application:

Notes:

Summary of What I Learned

Important Locations:

Memory Verse

Key Words:

Key People:

Questions:

IT'S ALL ABOUT JESUS

Weekly Prayer

My Prayer Focus:

My praise and worship
_____
_____
_____
_____

Lord I am grateful for...
_____
_____
_____
_____

Lord teach me to....
_____
_____
_____
_____

What are the struggles I am facing?
_____
_____
_____
_____

What may be God's answer to my prayer?
_____
_____
_____
_____

Prayer:
_____
_____
_____
_____
_____
_____
_____
_____
_____
_____
_____
_____
_____
_____
_____
_____
_____
_____
_____
_____
_____
_____
_____
_____
_____

Weekly Revelation

How did the Lord speak to me?
_____
_____
_____
_____
_____

Discription of what I saw/heard:

How do I feel about this revelation?
_____
_____
_____
_____
_____
_____

What may be the interpretation?
_____
_____
_____
_____
_____
_____
_____
_____
_____
_____

Biblical References:
- _____
- _____
- _____
- _____
- _____

IT'S ALL ABOUT JESUS

Weekly Self-Reflection

Verse:_____ Topic:_____

What's the context?

_____
_____
_____

My initial thoughts:

_____
_____
_____

Similar Verses:

- _____
- _____
- _____
- _____
- _____
- _____

What immediately stands out to me about this verse?

_____
_____
_____
_____

Does this show me how Christians are supposed to live?

_____
_____
_____
_____

Is there an example of this verse in the first 5 books of the Bible?

_____
_____
_____
_____

Does this remind me of anything Jesus said or did?

_____
_____
_____
_____

Weekly Self-Reflection

Question I am pondering about today:

IT'S ALL ABOUT JESUS

Self-Reflection Journal Prompts

1. What is God asking me to prioritize over the upcoming six months?
2. Today, God has given me someone to pray for.
3. Is my behavior this week indicating that I'm content with my life circumstances?
4. Who is God urging me to let go of my grudge against?
5. What aspects of the fruit of the Spirit do I need to enlist assistance in developing?
6. How can I help others by shining a light in a dark place?
7. Is there a time when I feel the most distant from the Lord?
8. How is my arrogance driving me to cause harm to others?
9. Do I find it difficult to communicate my regrets? If that's the case, why?
10. Choose a Biblical figure. What can I glean from their narrative?
11. What or who do I fear? Why?
12. How does God want me to listen to him?
13. What is the "next step" for my spiritual growth?
14. Am I pleasing God in my singleness/ married life/ as a parent?
15. Is there anything in my life that I should put my trust in the Lord for?
16. Describe the three most vulnerable areas of myself.
17. Describe three occasions in my life when the Lord provided for me and served as my protection.
18. According to Ecclesiastes, there is a season for everything. Which season am I now in?
19. Write my own Psalm of praise/thanksgiving to God.
20. When did Jesus Christ become my Lord and Savior?
21. How might I live within the anointing of the Lord?
22. Recall a period in my life when the Lord delivered me.
23. In my perspective, what will heaven be like?
24. What might I do this year to improve my patience?
25. How could I become more grateful this year?
26. Is it possible that I'm growing arrogant in some way? How can I make it right?
27. How can I make this year more enjoyable?
28. How can I make this year a more peaceful one for myself?
29. What could I do this year to cultivate obedience to the Lord?
30. How can I love more this year?
31. How can I become nicer and gentler this year?
32. Write a letter of forgiveness to an enemy.
33. If I am struggling with something, what do I think God wants me to learn from it?
34. What spiritual gifts do I possess? What can I do with them to further God's kingdom?
35. Write on a time when the Lord spoke to me.
36. Be still and listen. What is the Lord revealing to me at this moment?
37. When do I most strongly feel God's presence? What can I do when I don't feel His presence near?
38. The last time something angered me, how did I react to it? What does the reply reveal about my character?
39. How does my pride respond when something offends me?
40. How can I experience the Lord's healing in my life?
41. Who is one individual I can specifically help? How?
42. What steals my peace by diverting my thoughts from God?
43. When have I sensed God's grasp and presence lifting me up?
44. What component of my relationship with the Lord makes me the most thankful?
45. Which Bible scripture is my favorite, and why?
46. Do I just celebrate when things are going well? Can I celebrate while in famine?
47. What transgressions must I repent of to the Lord?
48. Make a list of song lyrics that speak to me and explain why.
49. What has been the greatest blessing so far in my life?
50. What am I sensing God calling me to change in my life?

June

"Truthless times need timeless truths."
-Mark Driscoll

June

1. _____
2. _____
3. _____
4. _____
5. _____
6. _____
7. _____
8. _____
9. _____
10. _____
11. _____
12. _____
13. _____
14. _____
15. _____
16. _____
17. _____
18. _____
19. _____
20. _____
21. _____
22. _____
23. _____
24. _____
25. _____
26. _____
27. _____
28. _____
29. _____
30. _____

Monthly Intention	Monthly Reflection
This month's prayer focus:	What I'm thankful for this month:
To make this month great I will:	What I have learned about God:
What I'm looking forward to this month:	Who I served this month:

Weekly Bible Goals/Faith In Action

Date: _____

Sunday	
Monday	
Tuesday	
Wednesday	
Thursday	
Friday	
Saturday	

IT'S ALL ABOUT JESUS

Weekly Reflection

Before I Start My Week:

What am I grateful for?

What does God want me to do this week?

What area do I want God to bless me?

How can I be Salt & Light to my community?

After My Week Ends:

How did I see God working in me?

Was I honoring God with my actions?

What things could I have done differently?

How did I reflect Christ's love this week?

Scripture Studied

Author:_____   Where:_____

When:_____   Why:_____

Scripture:

Cross Reverences::

Observation:

Application:

Notes:

Summary of What I Learned

Important Locations:

Memory Verse

Key Words:

Questions:

Key People:

Weekly Prayer

My Prayer Focus:

My praise and worship

_____
_____
_____
_____

Lord I am grateful for...

_____
_____
_____
_____

Lord teach me to....

_____
_____
_____
_____

What are the struggles I am facing?

_____
_____
_____
_____

What may be God's answer to my prayer?

_____
_____
_____
_____

Prayer:

_____
_____
_____
_____
_____
_____
_____
_____
_____
_____
_____
_____
_____
_____
_____
_____
_____
_____
_____
_____
_____
_____
_____
_____
_____
_____

IT'S ALL ABOUT JESUS

Weekly Revelation

How did the Lord speak to me?
_____
_____
_____
_____

Discription of what I saw/heard:

How do I feel about this revelation?
_____
_____
_____
_____
_____

What may be the interpretation?
_____
_____
_____
_____
_____
_____
_____
_____
_____

Biblical References :
- _____
- _____
- _____
- _____
- _____

IT'S ALL ABOUT JESUS

Weekly Self-Reflection

Verse:_____ Topic:_____

What's the context?

_____
_____
_____
_____

My initial thoughts:

_____
_____
_____
_____

Similar Verses:

- _____
- _____
- _____
- _____
- _____
- _____

What immediately stands out to me about this verse?

_____
_____
_____
_____

Does this show me how Christians are supposed to live?

_____
_____
_____
_____

Is there an example of this verse in the first 5 books of the Bible?

_____
_____
_____
_____

Does this remind me of anything Jesus said or did?

_____
_____
_____
_____

IT'S ALL ABOUT JESUS

Weekly Self-Reflection

Question I am pondering about today:

Self-Reflection Journal Prompts

1. What is God asking me to prioritize over the upcoming six months?
2. Today, God has given me someone to pray for.
3. Is my behavior this week indicating that I'm content with my life circumstances?
4. Who is God urging me to let go of my grudge against?
5. What aspects of the fruit of the Spirit do I need to enlist assistance in developing?
6. How can I help others by shining a light in a dark place?
7. Is there a time when I feel the most distant from the Lord?
8. How is my arrogance driving me to cause harm to others?
9. Do I find it difficult to communicate my regrets? If that's the case, why?
10. Choose a Biblical figure. What can I glean from their narrative?
11. What or who do I fear? Why?
12. How does God want me to listen to him?
13. What is the "next step" for my spiritual growth?
14. Am I pleasing God in my singleness/ married life/ as a parent?
15. Is there anything in my life that I should put my trust in the Lord for?
16. Describe the three most vulnerable areas of myself.
17. Describe three occasions in my life when the Lord provided for me and served as my protection.
18. According to Ecclesiastes, there is a season for everything. Which season am I now in?
19. Write my own Psalm of praise/thanksgiving to God.
20. When did Jesus Christ become my Lord and Savior?
21. How might I live within the anointing of the Lord?
22. Recall a period in my life when the Lord delivered me.
23. In my perspective, what will heaven be like?
24. What might I do this year to improve my patience?
25. How could I become more grateful this year?
26. Is it possible that I'm growing arrogant in some way? How can I make it right?
27. How can I make this year more enjoyable?
28. How can I make this year a more peaceful one for myself?
29. What could I do this year to cultivate obedience to the Lord?
30. How can I love more this year?
31. How can I become nicer and gentler this year?
32. Write a letter of forgiveness to an enemy.
33. If I am struggling with something, what do I think God wants me to learn from it?
34. What spiritual gifts do I possess? What can I do with them to further God's kingdom?
35. Write on a time when the Lord spoke to me.
36. Be still and listen. What is the Lord revealing to me at this moment?
37. When do I most strongly feel God's presence? What can I do when I don't feel His presence near?
38. The last time something angered me, how did I react to it? What does the reply reveal about my character?
39. How does my pride respond when something offends me?
40. How can I experience the Lord's healing in my life?
41. Who is one individual I can specifically help? How?
42. What steals my peace by diverting my thoughts from God?
43. When have I sensed God's grasp and presence lifting me up?
44. What component of my relationship with the Lord makes me the most thankful?
45. Which Bible scripture is my favorite, and why?
46. Do I just celebrate when things are going well? Can I celebrate while in famine?
47. What transgressions must I repent of to the Lord?
48. Make a list of song lyrics that speak to me and explain why.
49. What has been the greatest blessing so far in my life?
50. What am I sensing God calling me to change in my life?

IT'S ALL ABOUT JESUS

Weekly Bible Goals/Faith In Action

Date: _____

Day	
Sunday	
Monday	
Tuesday	
Wednesday	
Thursday	
Friday	
Saturday	

Weekly Reflection

Before I Start My Week:

What am I grateful for?

What does God want me to do this week?

What area do I want God to bless me?

How can I be Salt & Light to my community?

After My Week Ends:

How did I see God working in me?

Was I honoring God with my actions?

What things could I have done differently?

How did I reflect Christ's love this week?

IT'S ALL ABOUT JESUS

Scripture Studied

Author:_____   Where:_____

When:_____   Why:_____

Scripture:

Cross Reverences::

Observation:

Application:

Notes:

Summary of What I Learned

Important Locations:

Memory Verse

Key Words:

Key People:

Questions:

IT'S ALL ABOUT JESUS

Weekly Prayer

My Prayer Focus:

My praise and worship

_____
_____
_____

Lord I am grateful for...

_____
_____
_____

Lord teach me to....

_____
_____
_____

What are the struggles I am facing?

_____
_____
_____

What may be God's answer to my prayer?

_____
_____
_____

Prayer:

_____
_____
_____
_____
_____
_____
_____
_____
_____
_____
_____
_____
_____
_____
_____
_____
_____
_____
_____
_____

IT'S ALL ABOUT JESUS

Weekly Revelation

How did the Lord speak to me?
_____
_____
_____
_____

Discription of what I saw/heard:

How do I feel about this revelation?
_____
_____
_____
_____
_____

What may be the interpretation?
_____
_____
_____
_____
_____
_____
_____
_____

Biblical References :
- _____
- _____
- _____
- _____
- _____

IT'S ALL ABOUT JESUS

Weekly Self-Reflection

Verse:_____   Topic:_____

What's the context?

_____
_____
_____

My initial thoughts:

_____
_____
_____

Similar Verses :
- _____
- _____
- _____
- _____
- _____
- _____

What immediately stands out to me about this verse?

_____
_____
_____
_____

Does this show me how Christians are supposed to live?

_____
_____
_____
_____

Is there an example of this verse in the first 5 books of the Bible?

_____
_____
_____
_____

Does this remind me of anything Jesus said or did?

_____
_____
_____
_____

Weekly Self-Reflection

Question I am pondering about today:

IT'S ALL ABOUT JESUS

Self-Reflection Journal Prompts

1. What is God asking me to prioritize over the upcoming six months?
2. Today, God has given me someone to pray for.
3. Is my behavior this week indicating that I'm content with my life circumstances?
4. Who is God urging me to let go of my grudge against?
5. What aspects of the fruit of the Spirit do I need to enlist assistance in developing?
6. How can I help others by shining a light in a dark place?
7. Is there a time when I feel the most distant from the Lord?
8. How is my arrogance driving me to cause harm to others?
9. Do I find it difficult to communicate my regrets? If that's the case, why?
10. Choose a Biblical figure. What can I glean from their narrative?
11. What or who do I fear? Why?
12. How does God want me to listen to him?
13. What is the "next step" for my spiritual growth?
14. Am I pleasing God in my singleness/ married life/ as a parent?
15. Is there anything in my life that I should put my trust in the Lord for?
16. Describe the three most vulnerable areas of myself.
17. Describe three occasions in my life when the Lord provided for me and served as my protection.
18. According to Ecclesiastes, there is a season for everything. Which season am I now in?
19. Write my own Psalm of praise/thanksgiving to God.
20. When did Jesus Christ become my Lord and Savior?
21. How might I live within the anointing of the Lord?
22. Recall a period in my life when the Lord delivered me.
23. In my perspective, what will heaven be like?
24. What might I do this year to improve my patience?
25. How could I become more grateful this year?
26. Is it possible that I'm growing arrogant in some way? How can I make it right?
27. How can I make this year more enjoyable?
28. How can I make this year a more peaceful one for myself?
29. What could I do this year to cultivate obedience to the Lord?
30. How can I love more this year?
31. How can I become nicer and gentler this year?
32. Write a letter of forgiveness to an enemy.
33. If I am struggling with something, what do I think God wants me to learn from it?
34. What spiritual gifts do I possess? What can I do with them to further God's kingdom?
35. Write on a time when the Lord spoke to me.
36. Be still and listen. What is the Lord revealing to me at this moment?
37. When do I most strongly feel God's presence? What can I do when I don't feel His presence near?
38. The last time something angered me, how did I react to it? What does the reply reveal about my character?
39. How does my pride respond when something offends me?
40. How can I experience the Lord's healing in my life?
41. Who is one individual I can specifically help? How?
42. What steals my peace by diverting my thoughts from God?
43. When have I sensed God's grasp and presence lifting me up?
44. What component of my relationship with the Lord makes me the most thankful?
45. Which Bible scripture is my favorite, and why?
46. Do I just celebrate when things are going well? Can I celebrate while in famine?
47. What transgressions must I repent of to the Lord?
48. Make a list of song lyrics that speak to me and explain why.
49. What has been the greatest blessing so far in my life?
50. What am I sensing God calling me to change in my life?

IT'S ALL ABOUT JESUS

Weekly Bible Goals/Faith In Action

Date: _____

Sunday	
Monday	
Tuesday	
Wednesday	
Thursday	
Friday	
Saturday	

IT'S ALL ABOUT JESUS

Weekly Reflection

Before I Start My Week:

What am I grateful for?

What does God want me to do this week?

What area do I want God to bless me?

How can I be Salt & Light to my community?

After My Week Ends:

How did I see God working in me?

Was I honoring God with my actions?

What things could I have done differently?

How did I reflect Christ's love this week?

Scripture Studied

Author:_____   Where:_____

When:_____   Why:_____

Scripture:

Cross Reverences::

Observation:

Application:

Notes:

IT'S ALL ABOUT JESUS

Summary of What I Learned

Important Locations:

Memory Verse

Key Words:

Key People:

Questions:

Weekly Prayer

My Prayer Focus:

My praise and worship

_____
_____
_____
_____

Lord I am grateful for...

_____
_____
_____
_____

Lord teach me to....

_____
_____
_____
_____

What are the struggles I am facing?

_____
_____
_____
_____

What may be God's answer to my prayer?

_____
_____
_____
_____

Prayer:

_____
_____
_____
_____
_____
_____
_____
_____
_____
_____
_____
_____
_____
_____
_____
_____
_____
_____
_____
_____
_____
_____
_____
_____
_____

IT'S ALL ABOUT JESUS

Weekly Revelation

How did the Lord speak to me?
_____
_____
_____
_____

Discription of what I saw/heard:

How do I feel about this revelation?
_____
_____
_____
_____

What may be the interpretation?
_____
_____
_____
_____
_____
_____
_____
_____

Biblical References :
- _____
- _____
- _____
- _____
- _____

IT'S ALL ABOUT JESUS

Weekly Self-Reflection

Verse:_____ Topic:_____

What's the context?
_____
_____
_____

My initial thoughts:
_____
_____
_____
_____

Similar Verses :
- _____
- _____
- _____
- _____
- _____
- _____

What immediately stands out to me about this verse?
_____
_____
_____
_____

Does this show me how Christians are supposed to live?
_____
_____
_____
_____

Is there an example of this verse in the first 5 books of the Bible?
_____
_____
_____
_____

Does this remind me of anything Jesus said or did?
_____
_____
_____
_____

IT'S ALL ABOUT JESUS

Weekly Self-Reflection

Question I am pondering about today:

Self-Reflection Journal Prompts

1. What is God asking me to prioritize over the upcoming six months?
2. Today, God has given me someone to pray for.
3. Is my behavior this week indicating that I'm content with my life circumstances?
4. Who is God urging me to let go of my grudge against?
5. What aspects of the fruit of the Spirit do I need to enlist assistance in developing?
6. How can I help others by shining a light in a dark place?
7. Is there a time when I feel the most distant from the Lord?
8. How is my arrogance driving me to cause harm to others?
9. Do I find it difficult to communicate my regrets? If that's the case, why?
10. Choose a Biblical figure. What can I glean from their narrative?
11. What or who do I fear? Why?
12. How does God want me to listen to him?
13. What is the "next step" for my spiritual growth?
14. Am I pleasing God in my singleness/ married life/ as a parent?
15. Is there anything in my life that I should put my trust in the Lord for?
16. Describe the three most vulnerable areas of myself.
17. Describe three occasions in my life when the Lord provided for me and served as my protection.
18. According to Ecclesiastes, there is a season for everything. Which season am I now in?
19. Write my own Psalm of praise/thanksgiving to God.
20. When did Jesus Christ become my Lord and Savior?
21. How might I live within the anointing of the Lord?
22. Recall a period in my life when the Lord delivered me.
23. In my perspective, what will heaven be like?
24. What might I do this year to improve my patience?
25. How could I become more grateful this year?
26. Is it possible that I'm growing arrogant in some way? How can I make it right?
27. How can I make this year more enjoyable?
28. How can I make this year a more peaceful one for myself?
29. What could I do this year to cultivate obedience to the Lord?
30. How can I love more this year?
31. How can I become nicer and gentler this year?
32. Write a letter of forgiveness to an enemy.
33. If I am struggling with something, what do I think God wants me to learn from it?
34. What spiritual gifts do I possess? What can I do with them to further God's kingdom?
35. Write on a time when the Lord spoke to me.
36. Be still and listen. What is the Lord revealing to me at this moment?
37. When do I most strongly feel God's presence? What can I do when I don't feel His presence near?
38. The last time something angered me, how did I react to it? What does the reply reveal about my character?
39. How does my pride respond when something offends me?
40. How can I experience the Lord's healing in my life?
41. Who is one individual I can specifically help? How?
42. What steals my peace by diverting my thoughts from God?
43. When have I sensed God's grasp and presence lifting me up?
44. What component of my relationship with the Lord makes me the most thankful?
45. Which Bible scripture is my favorite, and why?
46. Do I just celebrate when things are going well? Can I celebrate while in famine?
47. What transgressions must I repent of to the Lord?
48. Make a list of song lyrics that speak to me and explain why.
49. What has been the greatest blessing so far in my life?
50. What am I sensing God calling me to change in my life?

IT'S ALL ABOUT JESUS

Weekly Bible Goals/Faith In Action

Date: _____

Day	
Sunday	
Monday	
Tuesday	
Wednesday	
Thursday	
Friday	
Saturday	

Weekly Reflection

Before I Start My Week:	After My Week Ends:
What am I grateful for?	How did I see God working in me?
What does God want me to do this week?	Was I honoring God with my actions?
What area do I want God to bless me?	What things could I have done differently?
How can I be Salt & Light to my community?	How did I reflect Christ's love this week?

IT'S ALL ABOUT JESUS

Scripture Studied

Author:_____   Where:_____

When:_____   Why:_____

Scripture:

_____
_____
_____
_____
_____
_____

Cross Reverences::

_____
_____
_____
_____

Observation:

Application:

Notes:
_____
_____
_____
_____
_____

Summary of What I Learned

_____
_____
_____
_____
_____

Important Locations:

[ ]   [ ]   [ ]

Memory Verse
_____
_____
_____
_____
_____
_____
_____
_____
_____
_____
_____
_____

Key Words:
- _____
- _____
- _____
- _____
- _____

Questions:
-
-
- _____
- _____
- _____
- _____
- _____

Key People:
- _____
- _____
- _____
- _____

IT'S ALL ABOUT JESUS

Weekly Prayer

My Prayer Focus:

My praise and worship

_____
_____
_____
_____

Lord I am grateful for...

_____
_____
_____
_____

Lord teach me to....

_____
_____
_____
_____

What are the struggles I am facing?

_____
_____
_____
_____

What may be God's answer to my prayer?

_____
_____
_____
_____

Prayer:

_____
_____
_____
_____
_____
_____
_____
_____
_____
_____
_____
_____
_____
_____
_____
_____
_____
_____
_____
_____
_____
_____
_____
_____
_____
_____
_____
_____

Weekly Revelation

How did the Lord speak to me?
_____
_____
_____
_____
_____

Discription of what I saw/heard:

How do I feel about this revelation?
_____
_____
_____
_____
_____
_____

What may be the interpretation?
_____
_____
_____
_____
_____
_____
_____
_____
_____

Biblical References :
- _____
- _____
- _____
- _____
- _____

IT'S ALL ABOUT JESUS

Weekly Self-Reflection

Verse:_____ Topic:_____

What's the context?

_____
_____
_____

Similar Verses:
- _____
- _____
- _____
- _____

My initial thoughts:

_____
_____
_____

- _____
- _____

What immediately stands out to me about this verse?

_____
_____
_____
_____

Does this show me how Christians are supposed to live?

_____
_____
_____
_____

Is there an example of this verse in the first 5 books of the Bible?

_____
_____
_____
_____

Does this remind me of anything Jesus said or did?

_____
_____
_____
_____

IT'S ALL ABOUT JESUS

Weekly Self-Reflection

Question I am pondering about today:

IT'S ALL ABOUT JESUS

Self-Reflection Journal Prompts

1. What is God asking me to prioritize over the upcoming six months?
2. Today, God has given me someone to pray for.
3. Is my behavior this week indicating that I'm content with my life circumstances?
4. Who is God urging me to let go of my grudge against?
5. What aspects of the fruit of the Spirit do I need to enlist assistance in developing?
6. How can I help others by shining a light in a dark place?
7. Is there a time when I feel the most distant from the Lord?
8. How is my arrogance driving me to cause harm to others?
9. Do I find it difficult to communicate my regrets? If that's the case, why?
10. Choose a Biblical figure. What can I glean from their narrative?
11. What or who do I fear? Why?
12. How does God want me to listen to him?
13. What is the "next step" for my spiritual growth?
14. Am I pleasing God in my singleness/ married life/ as a parent?
15. Is there anything in my life that I should put my trust in the Lord for?
16. Describe the three most vulnerable areas of myself.
17. Describe three occasions in my life when the Lord provided for me and served as my protection.
18. According to Ecclesiastes, there is a season for everything. Which season am I now in?
19. Write my own Psalm of praise/thanksgiving to God.
20. When did Jesus Christ become my Lord and Savior?
21. How might I live within the anointing of the Lord?
22. Recall a period in my life when the Lord delivered me.
23. In my perspective, what will heaven be like?
24. What might I do this year to improve my patience?
25. How could I become more grateful this year?
26. Is it possible that I'm growing arrogant in some way? How can I make it right?
27. How can I make this year more enjoyable?
28. How can I make this year a more peaceful one for myself?
29. What could I do this year to cultivate obedience to the Lord?
30. How can I love more this year?
31. How can I become nicer and gentler this year?
32. Write a letter of forgiveness to an enemy.
33. If I am struggling with something, what do I think God wants me to learn from it?
34. What spiritual gifts do I possess? What can I do with them to further God's kingdom?
35. Write on a time when the Lord spoke to me.
36. Be still and listen. What is the Lord revealing to me at this moment?
37. When do I most strongly feel God's presence? What can I do when I don't feel His presence near?
38. The last time something angered me, how did I react to it? What does the reply reveal about my character?
39. How does my pride respond when something offends me?
40. How can I experience the Lord's healing in my life?
41. Who is one individual I can specifically help? How?
42. What steals my peace by diverting my thoughts from God?
43. When have I sensed God's grasp and presence lifting me up?
44. What component of my relationship with the Lord makes me the most thankful?
45. Which Bible scripture is my favorite, and why?
46. Do I just celebrate when things are going well? Can I celebrate while in famine?
47. What transgressions must I repent of to the Lord?
48. Make a list of song lyrics that speak to me and explain why.
49. What has been the greatest blessing so far in my life?
50. What am I sensing God calling me to change in my life?

July

"Study the Bible like a soldier on a mission, not a scholar on a sabbatical."
—Mark Driscoll

July

1. _____
2. _____
3. _____
4. _____
5. _____
6. _____
7. _____
8. _____
9. _____
10. _____
11. _____
12. _____
13. _____
14. _____
15. _____
16. _____
17. _____
18. _____
19. _____
20. _____
21. _____
22. _____
23. _____
24. _____
25. _____
26. _____
27. _____
28. _____
29. _____
30. _____
31. _____

Monthly Intention	Monthly Reflection
This month's prayer focus:	What I'm thankful for this month:
To make this month great I will:	What I have learned about God:
What I'm looking forward to this month:	Who I served this month:

Weekly Bible Goals/Faith In Action

Date: _____

Sunday	
Monday	
Tuesday	
Wednesday	
Thursday	
Friday	
Saturday	

IT'S ALL ABOUT JESUS

Weekly Reflection

Before I Start My Week:

What am I grateful for?

What does God want me to do this week?

What area do I want God to bless me?

How can I be Salt & Light to my community?

After My Week Ends:

How did I see God working in me?

Was I honoring God with my actions?

What things could I have done differently?

How did I reflect Christ's love this week?

IT'S ALL ABOUT JESUS

Scripture Studied

Author:_____ Where:_____

When:_____ Why:_____

Scripture:

Cross Reverences::

Observation:

Application:

Notes:

IT'S ALL ABOUT JESUS

Summary of What I Learned

Important Locations:

Memory Verse

Key Words:

Questions:

Key People:

Weekly Prayer

My Prayer Focus:

My praise and worship

_____
_____
_____
_____

Lord I am grateful for...

_____
_____
_____
_____

Lord teach me to....

_____
_____
_____
_____

What are the struggles I am facing?

_____
_____
_____
_____

What may be God's answer to my prayer?

_____
_____
_____
_____

Prayer:

_____
_____
_____
_____
_____
_____
_____
_____
_____
_____
_____
_____
_____
_____
_____
_____
_____
_____
_____
_____

IT'S ALL ABOUT JESUS

Weekly Revelation

How did the Lord speak to me?
_____
_____
_____
_____

Discription of what I saw/heard:

How do I feel about this revelation?
_____
_____
_____
_____

What may be the interpretation?
_____
_____
_____
_____
_____
_____
_____
_____

Biblical References:
- _____
- _____
- _____
- _____
- _____

IT'S ALL ABOUT JESUS

Weekly Self-Reflection

Verse:_____   Topic:_____

What's the context?   Similar Verses:
_____   • _____
_____   • _____
_____   • _____

My initial thoughts: • _____
_____   • _____
_____   • _____
_____

What immediately stands out to me about this verse?
_____
_____
_____
_____

Does this show me how Christians are supposed to live?
_____
_____
_____
_____

Is there an example of this verse in the first 5 books of the Bible?
_____
_____
_____
_____

Does this remind me of anything Jesus said or did?
_____
_____
_____
_____

IT'S ALL ABOUT JESUS

Weekly Self-Reflection

Question I am pondering about today:

Self-Reflection Journal Prompts

1. What is God asking me to prioritize over the upcoming six months?
2. Today, God has given me someone to pray for.
3. Is my behavior this week indicating that I'm content with my life circumstances?
4. Who is God urging me to let go of my grudge against?
5. What aspects of the fruit of the Spirit do I need to enlist assistance in developing?
6. How can I help others by shining a light in a dark place?
7. Is there a time when I feel the most distant from the Lord?
8. How is my arrogance driving me to cause harm to others?
9. Do I find it difficult to communicate my regrets? If that's the case, why?
10. Choose a Biblical figure. What can I glean from their narrative?
11. What or who do I fear? Why?
12. How does God want me to listen to him?
13. What is the "next step" for my spiritual growth?
14. Am I pleasing God in my singleness/ married life/ as a parent?
15. Is there anything in my life that I should put my trust in the Lord for?
16. Describe the three most vulnerable areas of myself.
17. Describe three occasions in my life when the Lord provided for me and served as my protection.
18. According to Ecclesiastes, there is a season for everything. Which season am I now in?
19. Write my own Psalm of praise/thanksgiving to God.
20. When did Jesus Christ become my Lord and Savior?
21. How might I live within the anointing of the Lord?
22. Recall a period in my life when the Lord delivered me.
23. In my perspective, what will heaven be like?
24. What might I do this year to improve my patience?
25. How could I become more grateful this year?
26. Is it possible that I'm growing arrogant in some way? How can I make it right?
27. How can I make this year more enjoyable?
28. How can I make this year a more peaceful one for myself?
29. What could I do this year to cultivate obedience to the Lord?
30. How can I love more this year?
31. How can I become nicer and gentler this year?
32. Write a letter of forgiveness to an enemy.
33. If I am struggling with something, what do I think God wants me to learn from it?
34. What spiritual gifts do I possess? What can I do with them to further God's kingdom?
35. Write on a time when the Lord spoke to me.
36. Be still and listen. What is the Lord revealing to me at this moment?
37. When do I most strongly feel God's presence? What can I do when I don't feel His presence near?
38. The last time something angered me, how did I react to it? What does the reply reveal about my character?
39. How does my pride respond when something offends me?
40. How can I experience the Lord's healing in my life?
41. Who is one individual I can specifically help? How?
42. What steals my peace by diverting my thoughts from God?
43. When have I sensed God's grasp and presence lifting me up?
44. What component of my relationship with the Lord makes me the most thankful?
45. Which Bible scripture is my favorite, and why?
46. Do I just celebrate when things are going well? Can I celebrate while in famine?
47. What transgressions must I repent of to the Lord?
48. Make a list of song lyrics that speak to me and explain why.
49. What has been the greatest blessing so far in my life?
50. What am I sensing God calling me to change in my life?

IT'S ALL ABOUT JESUS

Weekly Bible Goals/Faith In Action

Date: _____

Day	
Sunday	
Monday	
Tuesday	
Wednesday	
Thursday	
Friday	
Saturday	

Weekly Reflection

Before I Start My Week:

What am I grateful for?

What does God want me to do this week?

What area do I want God to bless me?

How can I be Salt & Light to my community?

After My Week Ends:

How did I see God working in me?

Was I honoring God with my actions?

What things could I have done differently?

How did I reflect Christ's love this week?

IT'S ALL ABOUT JESUS

Scripture Studied

Author:_____ Where:_____

When:_____ Why:_____

Scripture:

Cross Reverences::

Observation:

Application:

Notes:

Summary of What I Learned

Important Locations:

Memory Verse

Key Words:

Questions:

Key People:

IT'S ALL ABOUT JESUS

Weekly Prayer

My Prayer Focus:

My praise and worship

_____
_____
_____
_____

Lord I am grateful for...

_____
_____
_____
_____

Lord teach me to....

_____
_____
_____
_____

What are the struggles I am facing?

_____
_____
_____
_____

What may be God's answer to my prayer?

_____
_____
_____
_____

Prayer:

_____
_____
_____
_____
_____
_____
_____
_____
_____
_____
_____
_____
_____
_____
_____
_____
_____
_____
_____
_____

Weekly Revelation

How did the Lord speak to me?
_____
_____
_____
_____
_____

Discription of what I saw/heard:

How do I feel about this revelation?
_____
_____
_____
_____
_____
_____

What may be the interpretation?
_____
_____
_____
_____
_____
_____
_____
_____
_____
_____

Biblical References :
- _____
- _____
- _____
- _____
- _____

IT'S ALL ABOUT JESUS

Weekly Self-Reflection

Verse:_____ Topic:_____

What's the context?
_____
_____
_____

My initial thoughts:
_____
_____
_____

Similar Verses :
- _____
- _____
- _____
- _____
- _____
- _____

What immediately stands out to me about this verse?
_____
_____
_____
_____

Does this show me how Christians are supposed to live?
_____
_____
_____
_____

Is there an example of this verse in the first 5 books of the Bible?
_____
_____
_____
_____

Does this remind me of anything Jesus said or did?
_____
_____
_____
_____

Weekly Self-Reflection

Question I am pondering about today:

IT'S ALL ABOUT JESUS

Self-Reflection Journal Prompts

1. What is God asking me to prioritize over the upcoming six months?
2. Today, God has given me someone to pray for.
3. Is my behavior this week indicating that I'm content with my life circumstances?
4. Who is God urging me to let go of my grudge against?
5. What aspects of the fruit of the Spirit do I need to enlist assistance in developing?
6. How can I help others by shining a light in a dark place?
7. Is there a time when I feel the most distant from the Lord?
8. How is my arrogance driving me to cause harm to others?
9. Do I find it difficult to communicate my regrets? If that's the case, why?
10. Choose a Biblical figure. What can I glean from their narrative?
11. What or who do I fear? Why?
12. How does God want me to listen to him?
13. What is the "next step" for my spiritual growth?
14. Am I pleasing God in my singleness/ married life/ as a parent?
15. Is there anything in my life that I should put my trust in the Lord for?
16. Describe the three most vulnerable areas of myself.
17. Describe three occasions in my life when the Lord provided for me and served as my protection.
18. According to Ecclesiastes, there is a season for everything. Which season am I now in?
19. Write my own Psalm of praise/thanksgiving to God.
20. When did Jesus Christ become my Lord and Savior?
21. How might I live within the anointing of the Lord?
22. Recall a period in my life when the Lord delivered me.
23. In my perspective, what will heaven be like?
24. What might I do this year to improve my patience?
25. How could I become more grateful this year?
26. Is it possible that I'm growing arrogant in some way? How can I make it right?
27. How can I make this year more enjoyable?
28. How can I make this year a more peaceful one for myself?
29. What could I do this year to cultivate obedience to the Lord?
30. How can I love more this year?
31. How can I become nicer and gentler this year?
32. Write a letter of forgiveness to an enemy.
33. If I am struggling with something, what do I think God wants me to learn from it?
34. What spiritual gifts do I possess? What can I do with them to further God's kingdom?
35. Write on a time when the Lord spoke to me.
36. Be still and listen. What is the Lord revealing to me at this moment?
37. When do I most strongly feel God's presence? What can I do when I don't feel His presence near?
38. The last time something angered me, how did I react to it? What does the reply reveal about my character?
39. How does my pride respond when something offends me?
40. How can I experience the Lord's healing in my life?
41. Who is one individual I can specifically help? How?
42. What steals my peace by diverting my thoughts from God?
43. When have I sensed God's grasp and presence lifting me up?
44. What component of my relationship with the Lord makes me the most thankful?
45. Which Bible scripture is my favorite, and why?
46. Do I just celebrate when things are going well? Can I celebrate while in famine?
47. What transgressions must I repent of to the Lord?
48. Make a list of song lyrics that speak to me and explain why.
49. What has been the greatest blessing so far in my life?
50. What am I sensing God calling me to change in my life?

Weekly Bible Goals/Faith In Action

Date: _____

Sunday	
Monday	
Tuesday	
Wednesday	
Thursday	
Friday	
Saturday	

IT'S ALL ABOUT JESUS

Weekly Reflection

Before I Start My Week:

What am I grateful for?

What does God want me to do this week?

What area do I want God to bless me?

How can I be Salt & Light to my community?

After My Week Ends:

How did I see God working in me?

Was I honoring God with my actions?

What things could I have done differently?

How did I reflect Christ's love this week?

IT'S ALL ABOUT JESUS

Scripture Studied

Author:_____   Where:_____

When:_____   Why:_____

Scripture:

Cross Reverences::

Observation:

Application:

Notes:

IT'S ALL ABOUT JESUS

Summary of What I Learned

Important Locations:

Memory Verse

Key Words:

Questions:

Key People:

Weekly Prayer

My Prayer Focus:

My praise and worship

Lord I am grateful for...

Lord teach me to....

What are the struggles I am facing?

What may be God's answer to my prayer?

Prayer:

IT'S ALL ABOUT JESUS

Weekly Revelation

How did the Lord speak to me?
_____
_____
_____
_____
_____

Discription of what I saw/heard:

How do I feel about this revelation?
_____
_____
_____
_____
_____

What may be the interpretation?
_____
_____
_____
_____
_____
_____
_____
_____

Biblical References :
- _____
- _____
- _____
- _____
- _____

IT'S ALL ABOUT JESUS

Weekly Self-Reflection

Verse:_____ Topic:_____

What's the context?

_____
_____
_____

My initial thoughts:

_____
_____
_____

Similar Verses:

- _____
- _____
- _____
- _____
- _____
- _____

What immediately stands out to me about this verse?

_____
_____
_____
_____

Does this show me how Christians are supposed to live?

_____
_____
_____
_____
_____

Is there an example of this verse in the first 5 books of the Bible?

_____
_____
_____
_____

Does this remind me of anything Jesus said or did?

_____
_____
_____
_____

IT'S ALL ABOUT JESUS

Weekly Self-Reflection

Question I am pondering about today:

Self-Reflection Journal Prompts

1. What is God asking me to prioritize over the upcoming six months?
2. Today, God has given me someone to pray for.
3. Is my behavior this week indicating that I'm content with my life circumstances?
4. Who is God urging me to let go of my grudge against?
5. What aspects of the fruit of the Spirit do I need to enlist assistance in developing?
6. How can I help others by shining a light in a dark place?
7. Is there a time when I feel the most distant from the Lord?
8. How is my arrogance driving me to cause harm to others?
9. Do I find it difficult to communicate my regrets? If that's the case, why?
10. Choose a Biblical figure. What can I glean from their narrative?
11. What or who do I fear? Why?
12. How does God want me to listen to him?
13. What is the "next step" for my spiritual growth?
14. Am I pleasing God in my singleness/ married life/ as a parent?
15. Is there anything in my life that I should put my trust in the Lord for?
16. Describe the three most vulnerable areas of myself.
17. Describe three occasions in my life when the Lord provided for me and served as my protection.
18. According to Ecclesiastes, there is a season for everything. Which season am I now in?
19. Write my own Psalm of praise/thanksgiving to God.
20. When did Jesus Christ become my Lord and Savior?
21. How might I live within the anointing of the Lord?
22. Recall a period in my life when the Lord delivered me.
23. In my perspective, what will heaven be like?
24. What might I do this year to improve my patience?
25. How could I become more grateful this year?
26. Is it possible that I'm growing arrogant in some way? How can I make it right?
27. How can I make this year more enjoyable?
28. How can I make this year a more peaceful one for myself?
29. What could I do this year to cultivate obedience to the Lord?
30. How can I love more this year?
31. How can I become nicer and gentler this year?
32. Write a letter of forgiveness to an enemy.
33. If I am struggling with something, what do I think God wants me to learn from it?
34. What spiritual gifts do I possess? What can I do with them to further God's kingdom?
35. Write on a time when the Lord spoke to me.
36. Be still and listen. What is the Lord revealing to me at this moment?
37. When do I most strongly feel God's presence? What can I do when I don't feel His presence near?
38. The last time something angered me, how did I react to it? What does the reply reveal about my character?
39. How does my pride respond when something offends me?
40. How can I experience the Lord's healing in my life?
41. Who is one individual I can specifically help? How?
42. What steals my peace by diverting my thoughts from God?
43. When have I sensed God's grasp and presence lifting me up?
44. What component of my relationship with the Lord makes me the most thankful?
45. Which Bible scripture is my favorite, and why?
46. Do I just celebrate when things are going well? Can I celebrate while in famine?
47. What transgressions must I repent of to the Lord?
48. Make a list of song lyrics that speak to me and explain why.
49. What has been the greatest blessing so far in my life?
50. What am I sensing God calling me to change in my life?

IT'S ALL ABOUT JESUS

Weekly Bible Goals/Faith In Action

Date: _____

Day	
Sunday	
Monday	
Tuesday	
Wednesday	
Thursday	
Friday	
Saturday	

Weekly Reflection

Before I Start My Week:

What am I grateful for?

What does God want me to do this week?

What area do I want God to bless me?

How can I be Salt & Light to my community?

After My Week Ends:

How did I see God working in me?

Was I honoring God with my actions?

What things could I have done differently?

How did I reflect Christ's love this week?

IT'S ALL ABOUT JESUS

Scripture Studied

Author:_____   Where:_____

When:_____   Why:_____

Scripture:

Cross Reverences::

Observation:

Application:

Notes:

Summary of What I Learned

Important Locations:

Memory Verse

Key Words:

Key People:

Questions:

IT'S ALL ABOUT JESUS

Weekly Prayer

My Prayer Focus:

My praise and worship

_____
_____
_____
_____

Lord I am grateful for...

_____
_____
_____
_____

Lord teach me to....

_____
_____
_____
_____

What are the struggles I am facing?

_____
_____
_____
_____

What may be God's answer to my prayer?

_____
_____
_____
_____

Prayer:

_____
_____
_____
_____
_____
_____
_____
_____
_____
_____
_____
_____
_____
_____
_____
_____
_____
_____
_____
_____

IT'S ALL ABOUT JESUS

Weekly Revelation

How did the Lord speak to me?
_____
_____
_____
_____
_____

Discription of what I saw/heard:

How do I feel about this revelation?
_____
_____
_____
_____
_____

What may be the interpretation?
_____
_____
_____
_____
_____
_____
_____
_____
_____

Biblical References :
- _____
- _____
- _____
- _____
- _____

IT'S ALL ABOUT JESUS

Weekly Self-Reflection

Verse:_____ Topic:_____

What's the context?
_____
_____
_____

My initial thoughts:
_____
_____
_____

Similar Verses:
- _____
- _____
- _____
- _____
- _____
- _____

What immediately stands out to me about this verse?
_____
_____
_____
_____

Does this show me how Christians are supposed to live?
_____
_____
_____
_____

Is there an example of this verse in the first 5 books of the Bible?
_____
_____
_____
_____

Does this remind me of anything Jesus said or did?
_____
_____
_____
_____

Weekly Self-Reflection

Question I am pondering about today:

IT'S ALL ABOUT JESUS

Self-Reflection Journal Prompts

1. What is God asking me to prioritize over the upcoming six months?
2. Today, God has given me someone to pray for.
3. Is my behavior this week indicating that I'm content with my life circumstances?
4. Who is God urging me to let go of my grudge against?
5. What aspects of the fruit of the Spirit do I need to enlist assistance in developing?
6. How can I help others by shining a light in a dark place?
7. Is there a time when I feel the most distant from the Lord?
8. How is my arrogance driving me to cause harm to others?
9. Do I find it difficult to communicate my regrets? If that's the case, why?
10. Choose a Biblical figure. What can I glean from their narrative?
11. What or who do I fear? Why?
12. How does God want me to listen to him?
13. What is the "next step" for my spiritual growth?
14. Am I pleasing God in my singleness/ married life/ as a parent?
15. Is there anything in my life that I should put my trust in the Lord for?
16. Describe the three most vulnerable areas of myself.
17. Describe three occasions in my life when the Lord provided for me and served as my protection.
18. According to Ecclesiastes, there is a season for everything. Which season am I now in?
19. Write my own Psalm of praise/thanksgiving to God.
20. When did Jesus Christ become my Lord and Savior?
21. How might I live within the anointing of the Lord?
22. Recall a period in my life when the Lord delivered me.
23. In my perspective, what will heaven be like?
24. What might I do this year to improve my patience?
25. How could I become more grateful this year?
26. Is it possible that I'm growing arrogant in some way? How can I make it right?
27. How can I make this year more enjoyable?
28. How can I make this year a more peaceful one for myself?
29. What could I do this year to cultivate obedience to the Lord?
30. How can I love more this year?
31. How can I become nicer and gentler this year?
32. Write a letter of forgiveness to an enemy.
33. If I am struggling with something, what do I think God wants me to learn from it?
34. What spiritual gifts do I possess? What can I do with them to further God's kingdom?
35. Write on a time when the Lord spoke to me.
36. Be still and listen. What is the Lord revealing to me at this moment?
37. When do I most strongly feel God's presence? What can I do when I don't feel His presence near?
38. The last time something angered me, how did I react to it? What does the reply reveal about my character?
39. How does my pride respond when something offends me?
40. How can I experience the Lord's healing in my life?
41. Who is one individual I can specifically help? How?
42. What steals my peace by diverting my thoughts from God?
43. When have I sensed God's grasp and presence lifting me up?
44. What component of my relationship with the Lord makes me the most thankful?
45. Which Bible scripture is my favorite, and why?
46. Do I just celebrate when things are going well? Can I celebrate while in famine?
47. What transgressions must I repent of to the Lord?
48. Make a list of song lyrics that speak to me and explain why.
49. What has been the greatest blessing so far in my life?
50. What am I sensing God calling me to change in my life?

August

"The Bible is not a book of principles to live by but rather a Person to live for."
—Mark Driscoll

August

1. _____
2. _____
3. _____
4. _____
5. _____
6. _____
7. _____
8. _____
9. _____
10. _____
11. _____
12. _____
13. _____
14. _____
15. _____
16. _____
17. _____
18. _____
19. _____
20. _____
21. _____
22. _____
23. _____
24. _____
25. _____
26. _____
27. _____
28. _____
29. _____
30. _____
31. _____

Monthly Intention	Monthly Reflection
This month's prayer focus:	What I'm thankful for this month:
To make this month great I will:	What I have learned about God:
What I'm looking forward to this month:	Who I served this month:

Weekly Bible Goals/Faith In Action

Date: _____

Sunday	
Monday	
Tuesday	
Wednesday	
Thursday	
Friday	
Saturday	

IT'S ALL ABOUT JESUS

Weekly Reflection

Before I Start My Week:

What am I grateful for?

What does God want me to do this week?

What area do I want God to bless me?

How can I be Salt & Light to my community?

After My Week Ends:

How did I see God working in me?

Was I honoring God with my actions?

What things could I have done differently?

How did I reflect Christ's love this week?

Scripture Studied

Author:_____ Where:_____

When:_____ Why:_____

Scripture:

Cross Reverences::

Observation:

Application:

Notes:
_____
_____
_____
_____
_____
_____

IT'S ALL ABOUT JESUS

Summary of What I Learned

Important Locations:

Memory Verse

Key Words:
-
-
-
-
-

Questions:
-
-
-
-
-

Key People:
-
-
-
-

Weekly Prayer

My Prayer Focus:

My praise and worship

Lord I am grateful for...

Lord teach me to....

What are the struggles I am facing?

What may be God's answer to my prayer?

Prayer:

IT'S ALL ABOUT JESUS

Weekly Revelation

How did the Lord speak to me?
_____
_____
_____
_____
_____

Discription of what I saw/heard:

How do I feel about this revelation?
_____
_____
_____
_____
_____

What may be the interpretation?
_____
_____
_____
_____
_____
_____
_____
_____
_____

Biblical References :
- _____
- _____
- _____
- _____
- _____

IT'S ALL ABOUT JESUS

Weekly Self-Reflection

Verse:_____ Topic:_____

What's the context?

_____
_____
_____

My initial thoughts:

_____
_____
_____

Similar Verses:

- _____
- _____
- _____
- _____
- _____
- _____

What immediately stands out to me about this verse?

_____
_____
_____
_____

Does this show me how Christians are supposed to live?

_____
_____
_____
_____

Is there an example of this verse in the first 5 books of the Bible?

_____
_____
_____
_____

Does this remind me of anything Jesus said or did?

_____
_____
_____
_____

IT'S ALL ABOUT JESUS

Weekly Self-Reflection

Question I am pondering about today:

Self-Reflection Journal Prompts

1. What is God asking me to prioritize over the upcoming six months?
2. Today, God has given me someone to pray for.
3. Is my behavior this week indicating that I'm content with my life circumstances?
4. Who is God urging me to let go of my grudge against?
5. What aspects of the fruit of the Spirit do I need to enlist assistance in developing?
6. How can I help others by shining a light in a dark place?
7. Is there a time when I feel the most distant from the Lord?
8. How is my arrogance driving me to cause harm to others?
9. Do I find it difficult to communicate my regrets? If that's the case, why?
10. Choose a Biblical figure. What can I glean from their narrative?
11. What or who do I fear? Why?
12. How does God want me to listen to him?
13. What is the "next step" for my spiritual growth?
14. Am I pleasing God in my singleness/ married life/ as a parent?
15. Is there anything in my life that I should put my trust in the Lord for?
16. Describe the three most vulnerable areas of myself.
17. Describe three occasions in my life when the Lord provided for me and served as my protection.
18. According to Ecclesiastes, there is a season for everything. Which season am I now in?
19. Write my own Psalm of praise/thanksgiving to God.
20. When did Jesus Christ become my Lord and Savior?
21. How might I live within the anointing of the Lord?
22. Recall a period in my life when the Lord delivered me.
23. In my perspective, what will heaven be like?
24. What might I do this year to improve my patience?
25. How could I become more grateful this year?
26. Is it possible that I'm growing arrogant in some way? How can I make it right?
27. How can I make this year more enjoyable?
28. How can I make this year a more peaceful one for myself?
29. What could I do this year to cultivate obedience to the Lord?
30. How can I love more this year?
31. How can I become nicer and gentler this year?
32. Write a letter of forgiveness to an enemy.
33. If I am struggling with something, what do I think God wants me to learn from it?
34. What spiritual gifts do I possess? What can I do with them to further God's kingdom?
35. Write on a time when the Lord spoke to me.
36. Be still and listen. What is the Lord revealing to me at this moment?
37. When do I most strongly feel God's presence? What can I do when I don't feel His presence near?
38. The last time something angered me, how did I react to it? What does the reply reveal about my character?
39. How does my pride respond when something offends me?
40. How can I experience the Lord's healing in my life?
41. Who is one individual I can specifically help? How?
42. What steals my peace by diverting my thoughts from God?
43. When have I sensed God's grasp and presence lifting me up?
44. What component of my relationship with the Lord makes me the most thankful?
45. Which Bible scripture is my favorite, and why?
46. Do I just celebrate when things are going well? Can I celebrate while in famine?
47. What transgressions must I repent of to the Lord?
48. Make a list of song lyrics that speak to me and explain why.
49. What has been the greatest blessing so far in my life?
50. What am I sensing God calling me to change in my life?

IT'S ALL ABOUT JESUS

Weekly Bible Goals/Faith In Action

Date: _____

Day	
Sunday	
Monday	
Tuesday	
Wednesday	
Thursday	
Friday	
Saturday	

Weekly Reflection

Before I Start My Week:

What am I grateful for?

What does God want me to do this week?

What area do I want God to bless me?

How can I be Salt & Light to my community?

After My Week Ends:

How did I see God working in me?

Was I honoring God with my actions?

What things could I have done differently?

How did I reflect Christ's love this week?

IT'S ALL ABOUT JESUS

Scripture Studied

Author:_____   Where:_____

When:_____   Why:_____

Scripture:

Cross Reverences::

Observation:

Application:

Notes:

Summary of What I Learned

Important Locations:

Memory Verse

Key Words:

Key People:

Questions:

IT'S ALL ABOUT JESUS

Weekly Prayer

My Prayer Focus:

My praise and worship

_____
_____
_____

Lord I am grateful for...

_____
_____
_____

Lord teach me to....

_____
_____
_____

What are the struggles I am facing?

_____
_____
_____

What may be God's answer to my prayer?

_____
_____
_____

Prayer:

_____
_____
_____
_____
_____
_____
_____
_____
_____
_____
_____
_____
_____
_____
_____
_____
_____
_____

Weekly Revelation

How did the Lord speak to me?
_____
_____
_____
_____
_____

Discription of what I saw/heard:

How do I feel about this revelation?
_____
_____
_____
_____
_____
_____

What may be the interpretation?
_____
_____
_____
_____
_____
_____
_____
_____
_____
_____

Biblical References:
- _____
- _____
- _____
- _____
- _____

IT'S ALL ABOUT JESUS

Weekly Self-Reflection

Verse:_____   Topic:_____

What's the context?
_____
_____
_____

My initial thoughts:
_____
_____
_____

Similar Verses :
- _____
- _____
- _____
- _____
- _____
- _____

What immediately stands out to me about this verse?
_____
_____
_____
_____

Does this show me how Christians are supposed to live?
_____
_____
_____
_____

Is there an example of this verse in the first 5 books of the Bible?
_____
_____
_____
_____

Does this remind me of anything Jesus said or did?
_____
_____
_____
_____

Weekly Self-Reflection

Question I am pondering about today:

IT'S ALL ABOUT JESUS

Self-Reflection Journal Prompts

1. What is God asking me to prioritize over the upcoming six months?
2. Today, God has given me someone to pray for.
3. Is my behavior this week indicating that I'm content with my life circumstances?
4. Who is God urging me to let go of my grudge against?
5. What aspects of the fruit of the Spirit do I need to enlist assistance in developing?
6. How can I help others by shining a light in a dark place?
7. Is there a time when I feel the most distant from the Lord?
8. How is my arrogance driving me to cause harm to others?
9. Do I find it difficult to communicate my regrets? If that's the case, why?
10. Choose a Biblical figure. What can I glean from their narrative?
11. What or who do I fear? Why?
12. How does God want me to listen to him?
13. What is the "next step" for my spiritual growth?
14. Am I pleasing God in my singleness/ married life/ as a parent?
15. Is there anything in my life that I should put my trust in the Lord for?
16. Describe the three most vulnerable areas of myself.
17. Describe three occasions in my life when the Lord provided for me and served as my protection.
18. According to Ecclesiastes, there is a season for everything. Which season am I now in?
19. Write my own Psalm of praise/thanksgiving to God.
20. When did Jesus Christ become my Lord and Savior?
21. How might I live within the anointing of the Lord?
22. Recall a period in my life when the Lord delivered me.
23. In my perspective, what will heaven be like?
24. What might I do this year to improve my patience?
25. How could I become more grateful this year?
26. Is it possible that I'm growing arrogant in some way? How can I make it right?
27. How can I make this year more enjoyable?
28. How can I make this year a more peaceful one for myself?
29. What could I do this year to cultivate obedience to the Lord?
30. How can I love more this year?
31. How can I become nicer and gentler this year?
32. Write a letter of forgiveness to an enemy.
33. If I am struggling with something, what do I think God wants me to learn from it?
34. What spiritual gifts do I possess? What can I do with them to further God's kingdom?
35. Write on a time when the Lord spoke to me.
36. Be still and listen. What is the Lord revealing to me at this moment?
37. When do I most strongly feel God's presence? What can I do when I don't feel His presence near?
38. The last time something angered me, how did I react to it? What does the reply reveal about my character?
39. How does my pride respond when something offends me?
40. How can I experience the Lord's healing in my life?
41. Who is one individual I can specifically help? How?
42. What steals my peace by diverting my thoughts from God?
43. When have I sensed God's grasp and presence lifting me up?
44. What component of my relationship with the Lord makes me the most thankful?
45. Which Bible scripture is my favorite, and why?
46. Do I just celebrate when things are going well? Can I celebrate while in famine?
47. What transgressions must I repent of to the Lord?
48. Make a list of song lyrics that speak to me and explain why.
49. What has been the greatest blessing so far in my life?
50. What am I sensing God calling me to change in my life?

Weekly Bible Goals/Faith In Action

Date: _____

Sunday	
Monday	
Tuesday	
Wednesday	
Thursday	
Friday	
Saturday	

IT'S ALL ABOUT JESUS

Weekly Reflection

Before I Start My Week:	After My Week Ends:
What am I grateful for?	How did I see God working in me?
What does God want me to do this week?	Was I honoring God with my actions?
What area do I want God to bless me?	What things could I have done differently?
How can I be Salt & Light to my community?	How did I reflect Christ's love this week?

Scripture Studied

Author: _____   Where: _____

When: _____   Why: _____

Scripture:

Cross Reverences::

Observation:

Application:

Notes:

IT'S ALL ABOUT JESUS

Summary of What I Learned

Important Locations:

Memory Verse

Key Words:

Questions:

Key People:

Weekly Prayer

My Prayer Focus:

My praise and worship

Lord I am grateful for...

Lord teach me to....

What are the struggles I am facing?

What may be God's answer to my prayer?

Prayer:

IT'S ALL ABOUT JESUS

Weekly Revelation

How did the Lord speak to me?
_____
_____
_____
_____

Discription of what I saw/heard:

How do I feel about this revelation?
_____
_____
_____
_____
_____

What may be the interpretation?
_____
_____
_____
_____
_____
_____
_____
_____
_____

Biblical References :
- _____
- _____
- _____
- _____
- _____

IT'S ALL ABOUT JESUS

Weekly Self-Reflection

Verse:_____   Topic:_____

What's the context?
_____
_____
_____

My initial thoughts:
_____
_____
_____
_____

Similar Verses:
- _____
- _____
- _____
- _____
- _____
- _____

What immediately stands out to me about this verse?
_____
_____
_____
_____

Does this show me how Christians are supposed to live?
_____
_____
_____
_____

Is there an example of this verse in the first 5 books of the Bible?
_____
_____
_____
_____

Does this remind me of anything Jesus said or did?
_____
_____
_____
_____

IT'S ALL ABOUT JESUS

Weekly Self-Reflection

Question I am pondering about today:

Self-Reflection Journal Prompts

1. What is God asking me to prioritize over the upcoming six months?
2. Today, God has given me someone to pray for.
3. Is my behavior this week indicating that I'm content with my life circumstances?
4. Who is God urging me to let go of my grudge against?
5. What aspects of the fruit of the Spirit do I need to enlist assistance in developing?
6. How can I help others by shining a light in a dark place?
7. Is there a time when I feel the most distant from the Lord?
8. How is my arrogance driving me to cause harm to others?
9. Do I find it difficult to communicate my regrets? If that's the case, why?
10. Choose a Biblical figure. What can I glean from their narrative?
11. What or who do I fear? Why?
12. How does God want me to listen to him?
13. What is the "next step" for my spiritual growth?
14. Am I pleasing God in my singleness/ married life/ as a parent?
15. Is there anything in my life that I should put my trust in the Lord for?
16. Describe the three most vulnerable areas of myself.
17. Describe three occasions in my life when the Lord provided for me and served as my protection.
18. According to Ecclesiastes, there is a season for everything. Which season am I now in?
19. Write my own Psalm of praise/thanksgiving to God.
20. When did Jesus Christ become my Lord and Savior?
21. How might I live within the anointing of the Lord?
22. Recall a period in my life when the Lord delivered me.
23. In my perspective, what will heaven be like?
24. What might I do this year to improve my patience?
25. How could I become more grateful this year?
26. Is it possible that I'm growing arrogant in some way? How can I make it right?
27. How can I make this year more enjoyable?
28. How can I make this year a more peaceful one for myself?
29. What could I do this year to cultivate obedience to the Lord?
30. How can I love more this year?
31. How can I become nicer and gentler this year?
32. Write a letter of forgiveness to an enemy.
33. If I am struggling with something, what do I think God wants me to learn from it?
34. What spiritual gifts do I possess? What can I do with them to further God's kingdom?
35. Write on a time when the Lord spoke to me.
36. Be still and listen. What is the Lord revealing to me at this moment?
37. When do I most strongly feel God's presence? What can I do when I don't feel His presence near?
38. The last time something angered me, how did I react to it? What does the reply reveal about my character?
39. How does my pride respond when something offends me?
40. How can I experience the Lord's healing in my life?
41. Who is one individual I can specifically help? How?
42. What steals my peace by diverting my thoughts from God?
43. When have I sensed God's grasp and presence lifting me up?
44. What component of my relationship with the Lord makes me the most thankful?
45. Which Bible scripture is my favorite, and why?
46. Do I just celebrate when things are going well? Can I celebrate while in famine?
47. What transgressions must I repent of to the Lord?
48. Make a list of song lyrics that speak to me and explain why.
49. What has been the greatest blessing so far in my life?
50. What am I sensing God calling me to change in my life?

IT'S ALL ABOUT JESUS

Weekly Bible Goals/Faith In Action

Date: _____

Sunday	
Monday	
Tuesday	
Wednesday	
Thursday	
Friday	
Saturday	

Weekly Reflection

Before I Start My Week:

What am I grateful for?

What does God want me to do this week?

What area do I want God to bless me?

How can I be Salt & Light to my community?

After My Week Ends:

How did I see God working in me?

Was I honoring God with my actions?

What things could I have done differently?

How did I reflect Christ's love this week?

IT'S ALL ABOUT JESUS

Scripture Studied

Author:_____ Where:_____

When:_____ Why:_____

Scripture:

Cross Reverences::

Observation:

Application:

Notes:

Summary of What I Learned

Important Locations:

Memory Verse

Key Words:

Questions:

Key People:

IT'S ALL ABOUT JESUS

Weekly Prayer

My Prayer Focus:

My praise and worship

Lord I am grateful for...

Lord teach me to....

What are the struggles I am facing?

What may be God's answer to my prayer?

Prayer:

Weekly Revelation

How did the Lord speak to me?
_____
_____
_____
_____
_____

Discription of what I saw/heard:

How do I feel about this revelation?
_____
_____
_____
_____
_____
_____

What may be the interpretation?
_____
_____
_____
_____
_____
_____
_____
_____
_____
_____

Biblical References:
- _____
- _____
- _____
- _____
- _____

IT'S ALL ABOUT JESUS

Weekly Self-Reflection

Verse:_____   Topic:_____

What's the context?

_____
_____
_____

My initial thoughts:

_____
_____
_____

Similar Verses :

- _____
- _____
- _____
- _____
- _____
- _____

What immediately stands out to me about this verse?

_____
_____
_____
_____

Does this show me how Christians are supposed to live?

_____
_____
_____
_____

Is there an example of this verse in the first 5 books of the Bible?

_____
_____
_____
_____

Does this remind me of anything Jesus said or did?

_____
_____
_____
_____

Weekly Self-Reflection

Question I am pondering about today:

IT'S ALL ABOUT JESUS

Self-Reflection Journal Prompts

1. What is God asking me to prioritize over the upcoming six months?
2. Today, God has given me someone to pray for.
3. Is my behavior this week indicating that I'm content with my life circumstances?
4. Who is God urging me to let go of my grudge against?
5. What aspects of the fruit of the Spirit do I need to enlist assistance in developing?
6. How can I help others by shining a light in a dark place?
7. Is there a time when I feel the most distant from the Lord?
8. How is my arrogance driving me to cause harm to others?
9. Do I find it difficult to communicate my regrets? If that's the case, why?
10. Choose a Biblical figure. What can I glean from their narrative?
11. What or who do I fear? Why?
12. How does God want me to listen to him?
13. What is the "next step" for my spiritual growth?
14. Am I pleasing God in my singleness/ married life/ as a parent?
15. Is there anything in my life that I should put my trust in the Lord for?
16. Describe the three most vulnerable areas of myself.
17. Describe three occasions in my life when the Lord provided for me and served as my protection.
18. According to Ecclesiastes, there is a season for everything. Which season am I now in?
19. Write my own Psalm of praise/thanksgiving to God.
20. When did Jesus Christ become my Lord and Savior?
21. How might I live within the anointing of the Lord?
22. Recall a period in my life when the Lord delivered me.
23. In my perspective, what will heaven be like?
24. What might I do this year to improve my patience?
25. How could I become more grateful this year?
26. Is it possible that I'm growing arrogant in some way? How can I make it right?
27. How can I make this year more enjoyable?
28. How can I make this year a more peaceful one for myself?
29. What could I do this year to cultivate obedience to the Lord?
30. How can I love more this year?
31. How can I become nicer and gentler this year?
32. Write a letter of forgiveness to an enemy.
33. If I am struggling with something, what do I think God wants me to learn from it?
34. What spiritual gifts do I possess? What can I do with them to further God's kingdom?
35. Write on a time when the Lord spoke to me.
36. Be still and listen. What is the Lord revealing to me at this moment?
37. When do I most strongly feel God's presence? What can I do when I don't feel His presence near?
38. The last time something angered me, how did I react to it? What does the reply reveal about my character?
39. How does my pride respond when something offends me?
40. How can I experience the Lord's healing in my life?
41. Who is one individual I can specifically help? How?
42. What steals my peace by diverting my thoughts from God?
43. When have I sensed God's grasp and presence lifting me up?
44. What component of my relationship with the Lord makes me the most thankful?
45. Which Bible scripture is my favorite, and why?
46. Do I just celebrate when things are going well? Can I celebrate while in famine?
47. What transgressions must I repent of to the Lord?
48. Make a list of song lyrics that speak to me and explain why.
49. What has been the greatest blessing so far in my life?
50. What am I sensing God calling me to change in my life?

September

"I study the Bible all week, pray to the Lord, and then I speak from my heart. It's all about brutal honesty."
—Mark Driscoll

September

1. _____
2. _____
3. _____
4. _____
5. _____
6. _____
7. _____
8. _____
9. _____
10. _____
11. _____
12. _____
13. _____
14. _____
15. _____
16. _____
17. _____
18. _____
19. _____
20. _____
21. _____
22. _____
23. _____
24. _____
25. _____
26. _____
27. _____
28. _____
29. _____
30. _____

Monthly Intention	Monthly Reflection
This month's prayer focus:	What I'm thankful for this month:
To make this month great I will:	What I have learned about God:
What I'm looking forward to this month:	Who I served this month:

Weekly Bible Goals/Faith In Action

Date: _____

Sunday	
Monday	
Tuesday	
Wednesday	
Thursday	
Friday	
Saturday	

IT'S ALL ABOUT JESUS

Weekly Reflection

Before I Start My Week:

What am I grateful for?

What does God want me to do this week?

What area do I want God to bless me?

How can I be Salt & Light to my community?

After My Week Ends:

How did I see God working in me?

Was I honoring God with my actions?

What things could I have done differently?

How did I reflect Christ's love this week?

Scripture Studied

Author:_____   Where:_____

When:_____   Why:_____

Scripture:

Cross Reverences::

Observation:

Application:

Notes:

IT'S ALL ABOUT JESUS

Summary of What I Learned

Important Locations:

Memory Verse

Key Words:

Questions:

Key People:

Weekly Prayer

My Prayer Focus:

My praise and worship

_____
_____
_____

Lord I am grateful for...

_____
_____
_____

Lord teach me to....

_____
_____
_____

What are the struggles I am facing?

_____
_____
_____

What may be God's answer to my prayer?

_____
_____
_____

Prayer:

_____
_____
_____
_____
_____
_____
_____
_____
_____
_____
_____
_____
_____
_____
_____
_____
_____
_____
_____
_____

IT'S ALL ABOUT JESUS

Weekly Revelation

How did the Lord speak to me?
_____
_____
_____
_____
_____

Discription of what I saw/heard:

How do I feel about this revelation?
_____
_____
_____
_____
_____

What may be the interpretation?
_____
_____
_____
_____
_____
_____
_____
_____
_____

Biblical References :
- _____
- _____
- _____
- _____
- _____

IT'S ALL ABOUT JESUS

Weekly Self-Reflection

Verse:_____   Topic:_____

What's the context?

_____
_____
_____

My initial thoughts:

_____
_____
_____
_____

Similar Verses:

- _____
- _____
- _____
- _____
- _____
- _____

What immediately stands out to me about this verse?

_____
_____
_____
_____

Does this show me how Christians are supposed to live?

_____
_____
_____
_____

Is there an example of this verse in the first 5 books of the Bible?

_____
_____
_____
_____

Does this remind me of anything Jesus said or did?

_____
_____
_____
_____

IT'S ALL ABOUT JESUS

Weekly Self-Reflection

Question I am pondering about today:

Self-Reflection Journal Prompts

1. What is God asking me to prioritize over the upcoming six months?
2. Today, God has given me someone to pray for.
3. Is my behavior this week indicating that I'm content with my life circumstances?
4. Who is God urging me to let go of my grudge against?
5. What aspects of the fruit of the Spirit do I need to enlist assistance in developing?
6. How can I help others by shining a light in a dark place?
7. Is there a time when I feel the most distant from the Lord?
8. How is my arrogance driving me to cause harm to others?
9. Do I find it difficult to communicate my regrets? If that's the case, why?
10. Choose a Biblical figure. What can I glean from their narrative?
11. What or who do I fear? Why?
12. How does God want me to listen to him?
13. What is the "next step" for my spiritual growth?
14. Am I pleasing God in my singleness/ married life/ as a parent?
15. Is there anything in my life that I should put my trust in the Lord for?
16. Describe the three most vulnerable areas of myself.
17. Describe three occasions in my life when the Lord provided for me and served as my protection.
18. According to Ecclesiastes, there is a season for everything. Which season am I now in?
19. Write my own Psalm of praise/thanksgiving to God.
20. When did Jesus Christ become my Lord and Savior?
21. How might I live within the anointing of the Lord?
22. Recall a period in my life when the Lord delivered me.
23. In my perspective, what will heaven be like?
24. What might I do this year to improve my patience?
25. How could I become more grateful this year?
26. Is it possible that I'm growing arrogant in some way? How can I make it right?
27. How can I make this year more enjoyable?
28. How can I make this year a more peaceful one for myself?
29. What could I do this year to cultivate obedience to the Lord?
30. How can I love more this year?
31. How can I become nicer and gentler this year?
32. Write a letter of forgiveness to an enemy.
33. If I am struggling with something, what do I think God wants me to learn from it?
34. What spiritual gifts do I possess? What can I do with them to further God's kingdom?
35. Write on a time when the Lord spoke to me.
36. Be still and listen. What is the Lord revealing to me at this moment?
37. When do I most strongly feel God's presence? What can I do when I don't feel His presence near?
38. The last time something angered me, how did I react to it? What does the reply reveal about my character?
39. How does my pride respond when something offends me?
40. How can I experience the Lord's healing in my life?
41. Who is one individual I can specifically help? How?
42. What steals my peace by diverting my thoughts from God?
43. When have I sensed God's grasp and presence lifting me up?
44. What component of my relationship with the Lord makes me the most thankful?
45. Which Bible scripture is my favorite, and why?
46. Do I just celebrate when things are going well? Can I celebrate while in famine?
47. What transgressions must I repent of to the Lord?
48. Make a list of song lyrics that speak to me and explain why.
49. What has been the greatest blessing so far in my life?
50. What am I sensing God calling me to change in my life?

IT'S ALL ABOUT JESUS

Weekly Bible Goals/Faith In Action

Date: _____

Day	
Sunday	
Monday	
Tuesday	
Wednesday	
Thursday	
Friday	
Saturday	

Weekly Reflection

Before I Start My Week:

What am I grateful for?

What does God want me to do this week?

What area do I want God to bless me?

How can I be Salt & Light to my community?

After My Week Ends:

How did I see God working in me?

Was I honoring God with my actions?

What things could I have done differently?

How did I reflect Christ's love this week?

IT'S ALL ABOUT JESUS

Scripture Studied

Author:_____ Where:_____

When:_____ Why:_____

Scripture:

Cross Reverences::

Observation:

Application:

Notes:

Summary of What I Learned

Important Locations:

Memory Verse

Key Words:

Key People:

Questions:

IT'S ALL ABOUT JESUS

Weekly Prayer

My Prayer Focus:

My praise and worship

_____
_____
_____

Lord I am grateful for...

_____
_____
_____

Lord teach me to....

_____
_____
_____

What are the struggles I am facing?

_____
_____
_____

What may be God's answer to my prayer?

_____
_____
_____

Prayer:

_____
_____
_____
_____
_____
_____
_____
_____
_____
_____
_____
_____
_____
_____
_____
_____
_____
_____
_____
_____

Weekly Revelation

How did the Lord speak to me?
_____
_____
_____
_____
_____

Discription of what I saw/heard:

How do I feel about this revelation?
_____
_____
_____
_____
_____
_____

What may be the interpretation?
_____
_____
_____
_____
_____
_____
_____
_____
_____

Biblical References :
- _____
- _____
- _____
- _____
- _____

IT'S ALL ABOUT JESUS

Weekly Self-Reflection

Verse:_____   Topic:_____

What's the context?

Similar Verses:

My initial thoughts:

What immediately stands out to me about this verse?

Does this show me how Christians are supposed to live?

Is there an example of this verse in the first 5 books of the Bible?

Does this remind me of anything Jesus said or did?

IT'S ALL ABOUT JESUS

Weekly Self-Reflection

Question I am pondering about today:

IT'S ALL ABOUT JESUS

Self-Reflection Journal Prompts

1. What is God asking me to prioritize over the upcoming six months?
2. Today, God has given me someone to pray for.
3. Is my behavior this week indicating that I'm content with my life circumstances?
4. Who is God urging me to let go of my grudge against?
5. What aspects of the fruit of the Spirit do I need to enlist assistance in developing?
6. How can I help others by shining a light in a dark place?
7. Is there a time when I feel the most distant from the Lord?
8. How is my arrogance driving me to cause harm to others?
9. Do I find it difficult to communicate my regrets? If that's the case, why?
10. Choose a Biblical figure. What can I glean from their narrative?
11. What or who do I fear? Why?
12. How does God want me to listen to him?
13. What is the "next step" for my spiritual growth?
14. Am I pleasing God in my singleness/ married life/ as a parent?
15. Is there anything in my life that I should put my trust in the Lord for?
16. Describe the three most vulnerable areas of myself.
17. Describe three occasions in my life when the Lord provided for me and served as my protection.
18. According to Ecclesiastes, there is a season for everything. Which season am I now in?
19. Write my own Psalm of praise/thanksgiving to God.
20. When did Jesus Christ become my Lord and Savior?
21. How might I live within the anointing of the Lord?
22. Recall a period in my life when the Lord delivered me.
23. In my perspective, what will heaven be like?
24. What might I do this year to improve my patience?
25. How could I become more grateful this year?
26. Is it possible that I'm growing arrogant in some way? How can I make it right?
27. How can I make this year more enjoyable?
28. How can I make this year a more peaceful one for myself?
29. What could I do this year to cultivate obedience to the Lord?
30. How can I love more this year?
31. How can I become nicer and gentler this year?
32. Write a letter of forgiveness to an enemy.
33. If I am struggling with something, what do I think God wants me to learn from it?
34. What spiritual gifts do I possess? What can I do with them to further God's kingdom?
35. Write on a time when the Lord spoke to me.
36. Be still and listen. What is the Lord revealing to me at this moment?
37. When do I most strongly feel God's presence? What can I do when I don't feel His presence near?
38. The last time something angered me, how did I react to it? What does the reply reveal about my character?
39. How does my pride respond when something offends me?
40. How can I experience the Lord's healing in my life?
41. Who is one individual I can specifically help? How?
42. What steals my peace by diverting my thoughts from God?
43. When have I sensed God's grasp and presence lifting me up?
44. What component of my relationship with the Lord makes me the most thankful?
45. Which Bible scripture is my favorite, and why?
46. Do I just celebrate when things are going well? Can I celebrate while in famine?
47. What transgressions must I repent of to the Lord?
48. Make a list of song lyrics that speak to me and explain why.
49. What has been the greatest blessing so far in my life?
50. What am I sensing God calling me to change in my life?

Weekly Bible Goals/Faith In Action

Date: _____

Sunday	
Monday	
Tuesday	
Wednesday	
Thursday	
Friday	
Saturday	

IT'S ALL ABOUT JESUS

Weekly Reflection

Before I Start My Week:	After My Week Ends:
What am I grateful for?	How did I see God working in me?
What does God want me to do this week?	Was I honoring God with my actions?
What area do I want God to bless me?	What things could I have done differently?
How can I be Salt & Light to my community?	How did I reflect Christ's love this week?

Scripture Studied

Author:_____ Where:_____

When:_____ Why:_____

Scripture:

Cross Reverences::

Observation:

Application:

Notes:

IT'S ALL ABOUT JESUS

Summary of What I Learned

Important Locations:

Memory Verse

Key Words:

Questions:

Key People:

Weekly Prayer

My Prayer Focus:

My praise and worship

_____
_____
_____
_____

Lord I am grateful for...

_____
_____
_____
_____

Lord teach me to....

_____
_____
_____
_____

What are the struggles I am facing?

_____
_____
_____
_____

What may be God's answer to my prayer?

_____
_____
_____
_____

Prayer:

_____
_____
_____
_____
_____
_____
_____
_____
_____
_____
_____
_____
_____
_____
_____
_____
_____
_____
_____
_____
_____
_____
_____
_____

IT'S ALL ABOUT JESUS

Weekly Revelation

How did the Lord speak to me?
_____
_____
_____
_____
_____

Discription of what I saw/heard:

How do I feel about this revelation?
_____
_____
_____
_____
_____
_____

What may be the interpretation?
_____
_____
_____
_____
_____
_____
_____
_____
_____
_____

Biblical References :
- _____
- _____
- _____
- _____
- _____

It's All About Jesus

Weekly Self-Reflection

Verse:_____   Topic:_____

What's the context?

_____
_____
_____
_____

Similar Verses :

- _____
- _____
- _____
- _____
- _____
- _____

My initial thoughts:

_____
_____
_____
_____

What immediately stands out to me about this verse?

_____
_____
_____
_____

Does this show me how Christians are supposed to live?

_____
_____
_____
_____

Is there an example of this verse in the first 5 books of the Bible?

_____
_____
_____
_____

Does this remind me of anything Jesus said or did?

_____
_____
_____
_____

IT'S ALL ABOUT JESUS

Weekly Self-Reflection

Question I am pondering about today:

Self-Reflection Journal Prompts

1. What is God asking me to prioritize over the upcoming six months?
2. Today, God has given me someone to pray for.
3. Is my behavior this week indicating that I'm content with my life circumstances?
4. Who is God urging me to let go of my grudge against?
5. What aspects of the fruit of the Spirit do I need to enlist assistance in developing?
6. How can I help others by shining a light in a dark place?
7. Is there a time when I feel the most distant from the Lord?
8. How is my arrogance driving me to cause harm to others?
9. Do I find it difficult to communicate my regrets? If that's the case, why?
10. Choose a Biblical figure. What can I glean from their narrative?
11. What or who do I fear? Why?
12. How does God want me to listen to him?
13. What is the "next step" for my spiritual growth?
14. Am I pleasing God in my singleness/ married life/ as a parent?
15. Is there anything in my life that I should put my trust in the Lord for?
16. Describe the three most vulnerable areas of myself.
17. Describe three occasions in my life when the Lord provided for me and served as my protection.
18. According to Ecclesiastes, there is a season for everything. Which season am I now in?
19. Write my own Psalm of praise/thanksgiving to God.
20. When did Jesus Christ become my Lord and Savior?
21. How might I live within the anointing of the Lord?
22. Recall a period in my life when the Lord delivered me.
23. In my perspective, what will heaven be like?
24. What might I do this year to improve my patience?
25. How could I become more grateful this year?
26. Is it possible that I'm growing arrogant in some way? How can I make it right?
27. How can I make this year more enjoyable?
28. How can I make this year a more peaceful one for myself?
29. What could I do this year to cultivate obedience to the Lord?
30. How can I love more this year?
31. How can I become nicer and gentler this year?
32. Write a letter of forgiveness to an enemy.
33. If I am struggling with something, what do I think God wants me to learn from it?
34. What spiritual gifts do I possess? What can I do with them to further God's kingdom?
35. Write on a time when the Lord spoke to me.
36. Be still and listen. What is the Lord revealing to me at this moment?
37. When do I most strongly feel God's presence? What can I do when I don't feel His presence near?
38. The last time something angered me, how did I react to it? What does the reply reveal about my character?
39. How does my pride respond when something offends me?
40. How can I experience the Lord's healing in my life?
41. Who is one individual I can specifically help? How?
42. What steals my peace by diverting my thoughts from God?
43. When have I sensed God's grasp and presence lifting me up?
44. What component of my relationship with the Lord makes me the most thankful?
45. Which Bible scripture is my favorite, and why?
46. Do I just celebrate when things are going well? Can I celebrate while in famine?
47. What transgressions must I repent of to the Lord?
48. Make a list of song lyrics that speak to me and explain why.
49. What has been the greatest blessing so far in my life?
50. What am I sensing God calling me to change in my life?

IT'S ALL ABOUT JESUS

Weekly Bible Goals/Faith In Action

Date: _____

Sunday	
Monday	
Tuesday	
Wednesday	
Thursday	
Friday	
Saturday	

Weekly Reflection

Before I Start My Week:

What am I grateful for?

What does God want me to do this week?

What area do I want God to bless me?

How can I be Salt & Light to my community?

After My Week Ends:

How did I see God working in me?

Was I honoring God with my actions?

What things could I have done differently?

How did I reflect Christ's love this week?

IT'S ALL ABOUT JESUS

Scripture Studied

Author:_____   Where:_____

When:_____   Why:_____

Scripture:

Cross Reverences::

Observation:

Application:

Notes:

Summary of What I Learned

Important Locations:

Memory Verse

Key Words:

Questions:

Key People:

IT'S ALL ABOUT JESUS

Weekly Prayer

My Prayer Focus:

My praise and worship

_____
_____
_____

Lord I am grateful for...

_____
_____
_____

Lord teach me to....

_____
_____
_____

What are the struggles I am facing?

_____
_____
_____

What may be God's answer to my prayer?

_____
_____
_____

Prayer:

_____
_____
_____
_____
_____
_____
_____
_____
_____
_____
_____
_____
_____
_____
_____
_____
_____
_____
_____
_____

Weekly Revelation

How did the Lord speak to me?
_____
_____
_____
_____

Discription of what I saw/heard:

How do I feel about this revelation?
_____
_____
_____
_____

What may be the interpretation?
_____
_____
_____
_____
_____
_____
_____

Biblical References:
- _____
- _____
- _____
- _____
- _____

IT'S ALL ABOUT JESUS

Weekly Self-Reflection

Verse:_____ Topic:_____

What's the context?

Similar Verses:

- _____
- _____
- _____
- _____
- _____
- _____

My initial thoughts:

What immediately stands out to me about this verse?

Does this show me how Christians are supposed to live?

Is there an example of this verse in the first 5 books of the Bible?

Does this remind me of anything Jesus said or did?

Weekly Self-Reflection

Question I am pondering about today:

IT'S ALL ABOUT JESUS

Self-Reflection Journal Prompts

1. What is God asking me to prioritize over the upcoming six months?
2. Today, God has given me someone to pray for.
3. Is my behavior this week indicating that I'm content with my life circumstances?
4. Who is God urging me to let go of my grudge against?
5. What aspects of the fruit of the Spirit do I need to enlist assistance in developing?
6. How can I help others by shining a light in a dark place?
7. Is there a time when I feel the most distant from the Lord?
8. How is my arrogance driving me to cause harm to others?
9. Do I find it difficult to communicate my regrets? If that's the case, why?
10. Choose a Biblical figure. What can I glean from their narrative?
11. What or who do I fear? Why?
12. How does God want me to listen to him?
13. What is the "next step" for my spiritual growth?
14. Am I pleasing God in my singleness/ married life/ as a parent?
15. Is there anything in my life that I should put my trust in the Lord for?
16. Describe the three most vulnerable areas of myself.
17. Describe three occasions in my life when the Lord provided for me and served as my protection.
18. According to Ecclesiastes, there is a season for everything. Which season am I now in?
19. Write my own Psalm of praise/thanksgiving to God.
20. When did Jesus Christ become my Lord and Savior?
21. How might I live within the anointing of the Lord?
22. Recall a period in my life when the Lord delivered me.
23. In my perspective, what will heaven be like?
24. What might I do this year to improve my patience?
25. How could I become more grateful this year?
26. Is it possible that I'm growing arrogant in some way? How can I make it right?
27. How can I make this year more enjoyable?
28. How can I make this year a more peaceful one for myself?
29. What could I do this year to cultivate obedience to the Lord?
30. How can I love more this year?
31. How can I become nicer and gentler this year?
32. Write a letter of forgiveness to an enemy.
33. If I am struggling with something, what do I think God wants me to learn from it?
34. What spiritual gifts do I possess? What can I do with them to further God's kingdom?
35. Write on a time when the Lord spoke to me.
36. Be still and listen. What is the Lord revealing to me at this moment?
37. When do I most strongly feel God's presence? What can I do when I don't feel His presence near?
38. The last time something angered me, how did I react to it? What does the reply reveal about my character?
39. How does my pride respond when something offends me?
40. How can I experience the Lord's healing in my life?
41. Who is one individual I can specifically help? How?
42. What steals my peace by diverting my thoughts from God?
43. When have I sensed God's grasp and presence lifting me up?
44. What component of my relationship with the Lord makes me the most thankful?
45. Which Bible scripture is my favorite, and why?
46. Do I just celebrate when things are going well? Can I celebrate while in famine?
47. What transgressions must I repent of to the Lord?
48. Make a list of song lyrics that speak to me and explain why.
49. What has been the greatest blessing so far in my life?
50. What am I sensing God calling me to change in my life?

IT'S ALL ABOUT JESUS

October

"If you really want to be a rebel get a job, cut your grass, read your bible, and shut up. Because no one is doing that."
-Mark Driscoll

October

1. _____
2. _____
3. _____
4. _____
5. _____
6. _____
7. _____
8. _____
9. _____
10. _____
11. _____
12. _____
13. _____
14. _____
15. _____
16. _____
17. _____
18. _____
19. _____
20. _____
21. _____
22. _____
23. _____
24. _____
25. _____
26. _____
27. _____
28. _____
29. _____
30. _____
31. _____

Monthly Intention	Monthly Reflection
This month's prayer focus:	What I'm thankful for this month:
To make this month great I will:	What I have learned about God:
What I'm looking forward to this month:	Who I served this month:

Weekly Bible Goals/Faith In Action

Date: _____

Sunday	
Monday	
Tuesday	
Wednesday	
Thursday	
Friday	
Saturday	

IT'S ALL ABOUT JESUS

Weekly Reflection

Before I Start My Week:	After My Week Ends:
What am I grateful for?	How did I see God working in me?
What does God want me to do this week?	Was I honoring God with my actions?
What area do I want God to bless me?	What things could I have done differently?
How can I be Salt & Light to my community?	How did I reflect Christ's love this week?

Scripture Studied

Author:_____ Where:_____

When:_____ Why:_____

Scripture:

Cross Reverences::

Observation:

Application:

Notes:
_____
_____
_____
_____
_____
_____

IT'S ALL ABOUT JESUS

Summary of What I Learned

Important Locations:

Memory Verse

Key Words:

Questions:

Key People:

IT'S ALL ABOUT JESUS

Weekly Prayer

My Prayer Focus:

My praise and worship

_____
_____
_____
_____
_____

Lord I am grateful for...

_____
_____
_____
_____

Lord teach me to....

_____
_____
_____
_____

What are the struggles I am facing?

_____
_____
_____
_____

What may be God's answer to my prayer?

_____
_____
_____
_____

Prayer:

_____
_____
_____
_____
_____
_____
_____
_____
_____
_____
_____
_____
_____
_____
_____
_____
_____
_____
_____
_____
_____
_____
_____
_____
_____
_____
_____
_____
_____

IT'S ALL ABOUT JESUS

Weekly Revelation

How did the Lord speak to me?
_____
_____
_____
_____
_____

Discription of what I saw/heard:

How do I feel about this revelation?
_____
_____
_____
_____
_____

What may be the interpretation?
_____
_____
_____
_____
_____
_____
_____
_____
_____

Biblical References :
- _____
- _____
- _____
- _____
- _____

IT'S ALL ABOUT JESUS

Weekly Self-Reflection

Verse:_____ Topic:_____

What's the context?
_____
_____
_____
_____

Similar Verses :
- _____
- _____
- _____
- _____
- _____
- _____

My initial thoughts:
_____
_____
_____
_____

What immediately stands out to me about this verse?
_____
_____
_____
_____

Does this show me how Christians are supposed to live?
_____
_____
_____
_____

Is there an example of this verse in the first 5 books of the Bible?
_____
_____
_____
_____

Does this remind me of anything Jesus said or did?
_____
_____
_____
_____

IT'S ALL ABOUT JESUS

Weekly Self-Reflection

Question I am pondering about today:

Self-Reflection Journal Prompts

1. What is God asking me to prioritize over the upcoming six months?
2. Today, God has given me someone to pray for.
3. Is my behavior this week indicating that I'm content with my life circumstances?
4. Who is God urging me to let go of my grudge against?
5. What aspects of the fruit of the Spirit do I need to enlist assistance in developing?
6. How can I help others by shining a light in a dark place?
7. Is there a time when I feel the most distant from the Lord?
8. How is my arrogance driving me to cause harm to others?
9. Do I find it difficult to communicate my regrets? If that's the case, why?
10. Choose a Biblical figure. What can I glean from their narrative?
11. What or who do I fear? Why?
12. How does God want me to listen to him?
13. What is the "next step" for my spiritual growth?
14. Am I pleasing God in my singleness/ married life/ as a parent?
15. Is there anything in my life that I should put my trust in the Lord for?
16. Describe the three most vulnerable areas of myself.
17. Describe three occasions in my life when the Lord provided for me and served as my protection.
18. According to Ecclesiastes, there is a season for everything. Which season am I now in?
19. Write my own Psalm of praise/thanksgiving to God.
20. When did Jesus Christ become my Lord and Savior?
21. How might I live within the anointing of the Lord?
22. Recall a period in my life when the Lord delivered me.
23. In my perspective, what will heaven be like?
24. What might I do this year to improve my patience?
25. How could I become more grateful this year?
26. Is it possible that I'm growing arrogant in some way? How can I make it right?
27. How can I make this year more enjoyable?
28. How can I make this year a more peaceful one for myself?
29. What could I do this year to cultivate obedience to the Lord?
30. How can I love more this year?
31. How can I become nicer and gentler this year?
32. Write a letter of forgiveness to an enemy.
33. If I am struggling with something, what do I think God wants me to learn from it?
34. What spiritual gifts do I possess? What can I do with them to further God's kingdom?
35. Write on a time when the Lord spoke to me.
36. Be still and listen. What is the Lord revealing to me at this moment?
37. When do I most strongly feel God's presence? What can I do when I don't feel His presence near?
38. The last time something angered me, how did I react to it? What does the reply reveal about my character?
39. How does my pride respond when something offends me?
40. How can I experience the Lord's healing in my life?
41. Who is one individual I can specifically help? How?
42. What steals my peace by diverting my thoughts from God?
43. When have I sensed God's grasp and presence lifting me up?
44. What component of my relationship with the Lord makes me the most thankful?
45. Which Bible scripture is my favorite, and why?
46. Do I just celebrate when things are going well? Can I celebrate while in famine?
47. What transgressions must I repent of to the Lord?
48. Make a list of song lyrics that speak to me and explain why.
49. What has been the greatest blessing so far in my life?
50. What am I sensing God calling me to change in my life?

IT'S ALL ABOUT JESUS

Weekly Bible Goals/Faith In Action

Date: _____

Day	
Sunday	
Monday	
Tuesday	
Wednesday	
Thursday	
Friday	
Saturday	

Weekly Reflection

Before I Start My Week:	After My Week Ends:
What am I grateful for?	How did I see God working in me?
What does God want me to do this week?	Was I honoring God with my actions?
What area do I want God to bless me?	What things could I have done differently?
How can I be Salt & Light to my community?	How did I reflect Christ's love this week?

IT'S ALL ABOUT JESUS

Scripture Studied

Author:_____   Where:_____

When:_____   Why:_____

Scripture:

Cross Reverences::

Observation:

Application:

Notes:

Summary of What I Learned

Important Locations:

Memory Verse

Key Words:

Key People:

Questions:

IT'S ALL ABOUT JESUS

Weekly Prayer

My Prayer Focus:

My praise and worship

Lord I am grateful for...

Lord teach me to....

What are the struggles I am facing?

What may be God's answer to my prayer?

Prayer:

Weekly Revelation

How did the Lord speak to me?
_____
_____
_____
_____

Discription of what I saw/heard:

How do I feel about this revelation?
_____
_____
_____
_____
_____

What may be the interpretation?
_____
_____
_____
_____
_____
_____
_____
_____

Biblical References :
- _____
- _____
- _____
- _____
- _____

IT'S ALL ABOUT JESUS

Weekly Self-Reflection

Verse:_____ Topic:_____

What's the context?

_____
_____
_____

My initial thoughts:

_____
_____
_____

Similar Verses:
- _____
- _____
- _____
- _____
- _____
- _____

What immediately stands out to me about this verse?

_____
_____
_____
_____

Does this show me how Christians are supposed to live?

_____
_____
_____
_____

Is there an example of this verse in the first 5 books of the Bible?

_____
_____
_____
_____

Does this remind me of anything Jesus said or did?

_____
_____
_____
_____

IT'S ALL ABOUT JESUS

Weekly Self-Reflection

Question I am pondering about today:

IT'S ALL ABOUT JESUS

Self-Reflection Journal Prompts

1. What is God asking me to prioritize over the upcoming six months?
2. Today, God has given me someone to pray for.
3. Is my behavior this week indicating that I'm content with my life circumstances?
4. Who is God urging me to let go of my grudge against?
5. What aspects of the fruit of the Spirit do I need to enlist assistance in developing?
6. How can I help others by shining a light in a dark place?
7. Is there a time when I feel the most distant from the Lord?
8. How is my arrogance driving me to cause harm to others?
9. Do I find it difficult to communicate my regrets? If that's the case, why?
10. Choose a Biblical figure. What can I glean from their narrative?
11. What or who do I fear? Why?
12. How does God want me to listen to him?
13. What is the "next step" for my spiritual growth?
14. Am I pleasing God in my singleness/ married life/ as a parent?
15. Is there anything in my life that I should put my trust in the Lord for?
16. Describe the three most vulnerable areas of myself.
17. Describe three occasions in my life when the Lord provided for me and served as my protection.
18. According to Ecclesiastes, there is a season for everything. Which season am I now in?
19. Write my own Psalm of praise/thanksgiving to God.
20. When did Jesus Christ become my Lord and Savior?
21. How might I live within the anointing of the Lord?
22. Recall a period in my life when the Lord delivered me.
23. In my perspective, what will heaven be like?
24. What might I do this year to improve my patience?
25. How could I become more grateful this year?
26. Is it possible that I'm growing arrogant in some way? How can I make it right?
27. How can I make this year more enjoyable?
28. How can I make this year a more peaceful one for myself?
29. What could I do this year to cultivate obedience to the Lord?
30. How can I love more this year?
31. How can I become nicer and gentler this year?
32. Write a letter of forgiveness to an enemy.
33. If I am struggling with something, what do I think God wants me to learn from it?
34. What spiritual gifts do I possess? What can I do with them to further God's kingdom?
35. Write on a time when the Lord spoke to me.
36. Be still and listen. What is the Lord revealing to me at this moment?
37. When do I most strongly feel God's presence? What can I do when I don't feel His presence near?
38. The last time something angered me, how did I react to it? What does the reply reveal about my character?
39. How does my pride respond when something offends me?
40. How can I experience the Lord's healing in my life?
41. Who is one individual I can specifically help? How?
42. What steals my peace by diverting my thoughts from God?
43. When have I sensed God's grasp and presence lifting me up?
44. What component of my relationship with the Lord makes me the most thankful?
45. Which Bible scripture is my favorite, and why?
46. Do I just celebrate when things are going well? Can I celebrate while in famine?
47. What transgressions must I repent of to the Lord?
48. Make a list of song lyrics that speak to me and explain why.
49. What has been the greatest blessing so far in my life?
50. What am I sensing God calling me to change in my life?

Weekly Bible Goals/Faith In Action

Date: _____

Sunday	
Monday	
Tuesday	
Wednesday	
Thursday	
Friday	
Saturday	

IT'S ALL ABOUT JESUS

Weekly Reflection

Before I Start My Week:	After My Week Ends:
What am I grateful for?	How did I see God working in me?
What does God want me to do this week?	Was I honoring God with my actions?
What area do I want God to bless me?	What things could I have done differently?
How can I be Salt & Light to my community?	How did I reflect Christ's love this week?

Scripture Studied

Author:_____ Where:_____

When:_____ Why:_____

Scripture:

Cross Reverences::

Observation:

Application:

Notes:

IT'S ALL ABOUT JESUS

Summary of What I Learned

Important Locations:

Memory Verse

Key Words:

Key People:

Questions:

IT'S ALL ABOUT JESUS

Weekly Prayer

My Prayer Focus:

My praise and worship

Lord I am grateful for...

Lord teach me to....

What are the struggles I am facing?

What may be God's answer to my prayer?

Prayer:

IT'S ALL ABOUT JESUS

Weekly Revelation

How did the Lord speak to me?

Discription of what I saw/heard:

How do I feel about this revelation?

What may be the interpretation?

Biblical References :
- _____
- _____
- _____
- _____
- _____

Weekly Self-Reflection

Verse:_____   Topic:_____

What's the context?
_____
_____
_____

My initial thoughts:
_____
_____
_____
_____

Similar Verses:
- _____
- _____
- _____
- _____
- _____
- _____

What immediately stands out to me about this verse?
_____
_____
_____
_____
_____

Does this show me how Christians are supposed to live?
_____
_____
_____
_____
_____

Is there an example of this verse in the first 5 books of the Bible?
_____
_____
_____
_____

Does this remind me of anything Jesus said or did?
_____
_____
_____
_____

IT'S ALL ABOUT JESUS

Weekly Self-Reflection

Question I am pondering about today:

Self-Reflection Journal Prompts

1. What is God asking me to prioritize over the upcoming six months?
2. Today, God has given me someone to pray for.
3. Is my behavior this week indicating that I'm content with my life circumstances?
4. Who is God urging me to let go of my grudge against?
5. What aspects of the fruit of the Spirit do I need to enlist assistance in developing?
6. How can I help others by shining a light in a dark place?
7. Is there a time when I feel the most distant from the Lord?
8. How is my arrogance driving me to cause harm to others?
9. Do I find it difficult to communicate my regrets? If that's the case, why?
10. Choose a Biblical figure. What can I glean from their narrative?
11. What or who do I fear? Why?
12. How does God want me to listen to him?
13. What is the "next step" for my spiritual growth?
14. Am I pleasing God in my singleness/ married life/ as a parent?
15. Is there anything in my life that I should put my trust in the Lord for?
16. Describe the three most vulnerable areas of myself.
17. Describe three occasions in my life when the Lord provided for me and served as my protection.
18. According to Ecclesiastes, there is a season for everything. Which season am I now in?
19. Write my own Psalm of praise/thanksgiving to God.
20. When did Jesus Christ become my Lord and Savior?
21. How might I live within the anointing of the Lord?
22. Recall a period in my life when the Lord delivered me.
23. In my perspective, what will heaven be like?
24. What might I do this year to improve my patience?
25. How could I become more grateful this year?
26. Is it possible that I'm growing arrogant in some way? How can I make it right?
27. How can I make this year more enjoyable?
28. How can I make this year a more peaceful one for myself?
29. What could I do this year to cultivate obedience to the Lord?
30. How can I love more this year?
31. How can I become nicer and gentler this year?
32. Write a letter of forgiveness to an enemy.
33. If I am struggling with something, what do I think God wants me to learn from it?
34. What spiritual gifts do I possess? What can I do with them to further God's kingdom?
35. Write on a time when the Lord spoke to me.
36. Be still and listen. What is the Lord revealing to me at this moment?
37. When do I most strongly feel God's presence? What can I do when I don't feel His presence near?
38. The last time something angered me, how did I react to it? What does the reply reveal about my character?
39. How does my pride respond when something offends me?
40. How can I experience the Lord's healing in my life?
41. Who is one individual I can specifically help? How?
42. What steals my peace by diverting my thoughts from God?
43. When have I sensed God's grasp and presence lifting me up?
44. What component of my relationship with the Lord makes me the most thankful?
45. Which Bible scripture is my favorite, and why?
46. Do I just celebrate when things are going well? Can I celebrate while in famine?
47. What transgressions must I repent of to the Lord?
48. Make a list of song lyrics that speak to me and explain why.
49. What has been the greatest blessing so far in my life?
50. What am I sensing God calling me to change in my life?

IT'S ALL ABOUT JESUS

Weekly Bible Goals/Faith In Action

Date: _____

Sunday	
Monday	
Tuesday	
Wednesday	
Thursday	
Friday	
Saturday	

Weekly Reflection

Before I Start My Week:

What am I grateful for?

What does God want me to do this week?

What area do I want God to bless me?

How can I be Salt & Light to my community?

After My Week Ends:

How did I see God working in me?

Was I honoring God with my actions?

What things could I have done differently?

How did I reflect Christ's love this week?

IT'S ALL ABOUT JESUS

Scripture Studied

Author:_____ Where:_____

When:_____ Why:_____

Scripture:

Cross Reverences::

Observation:

Application:

Notes:

Summary of What I Learned

Important Locations:

Memory Verse

Key Words:

Questions:

Key People:

IT'S ALL ABOUT JESUS

Weekly Prayer

My Prayer Focus:

My praise and worship
_____
_____
_____
_____

Lord I am grateful for...
_____
_____
_____
_____

Lord teach me to....
_____
_____
_____
_____

What are the struggles I am facing?
_____
_____
_____
_____

What may be God's answer to my prayer?
_____
_____
_____
_____

Prayer:
_____
_____
_____
_____
_____
_____
_____
_____
_____
_____
_____
_____
_____
_____
_____
_____
_____
_____
_____
_____

Weekly Revelation

How did the Lord speak to me?
_____
_____
_____
_____

Discription of what I saw/heard:

How do I feel about this revelation?
_____
_____
_____
_____
_____

What may be the interpretation?
_____
_____
_____
_____
_____
_____
_____
_____
_____

Biblical References:
- _____
- _____
- _____
- _____
- _____

IT'S ALL ABOUT JESUS

Weekly Self-Reflection

Verse:_____   Topic:_____

What's the context?
_____
_____
_____

Similar Verses :
- _____
- _____
- _____
- _____
- _____
- _____

My initial thoughts:
_____
_____
_____

What immediately stands out to me about this verse?
_____
_____
_____
_____

Does this show me how Christians are supposed to live?
_____
_____
_____
_____

Is there an example of this verse in the first 5 books of the Bible?
_____
_____
_____
_____

Does this remind me of anything Jesus said or did?
_____
_____
_____
_____

Weekly Self-Reflection

Question I am pondering about today:

IT'S ALL ABOUT JESUS

Self-Reflection Journal Prompts

1. What is God asking me to prioritize over the upcoming six months?
2. Today, God has given me someone to pray for.
3. Is my behavior this week indicating that I'm content with my life circumstances?
4. Who is God urging me to let go of my grudge against?
5. What aspects of the fruit of the Spirit do I need to enlist assistance in developing?
6. How can I help others by shining a light in a dark place?
7. Is there a time when I feel the most distant from the Lord?
8. How is my arrogance driving me to cause harm to others?
9. Do I find it difficult to communicate my regrets? If that's the case, why?
10. Choose a Biblical figure. What can I glean from their narrative?
11. What or who do I fear? Why?
12. How does God want me to listen to him?
13. What is the "next step" for my spiritual growth?
14. Am I pleasing God in my singleness/ married life/ as a parent?
15. Is there anything in my life that I should put my trust in the Lord for?
16. Describe the three most vulnerable areas of myself.
17. Describe three occasions in my life when the Lord provided for me and served as my protection.
18. According to Ecclesiastes, there is a season for everything. Which season am I now in?
19. Write my own Psalm of praise/thanksgiving to God.
20. When did Jesus Christ become my Lord and Savior?
21. How might I live within the anointing of the Lord?
22. Recall a period in my life when the Lord delivered me.
23. In my perspective, what will heaven be like?
24. What might I do this year to improve my patience?
25. How could I become more grateful this year?
26. Is it possible that I'm growing arrogant in some way? How can I make it right?
27. How can I make this year more enjoyable?
28. How can I make this year a more peaceful one for myself?
29. What could I do this year to cultivate obedience to the Lord?
30. How can I love more this year?
31. How can I become nicer and gentler this year?
32. Write a letter of forgiveness to an enemy.
33. If I am struggling with something, what do I think God wants me to learn from it?
34. What spiritual gifts do I possess? What can I do with them to further God's kingdom?
35. Write on a time when the Lord spoke to me.
36. Be still and listen. What is the Lord revealing to me at this moment?
37. When do I most strongly feel God's presence? What can I do when I don't feel His presence near?
38. The last time something angered me, how did I react to it? What does the reply reveal about my character?
39. How does my pride respond when something offends me?
40. How can I experience the Lord's healing in my life?
41. Who is one individual I can specifically help? How?
42. What steals my peace by diverting my thoughts from God?
43. When have I sensed God's grasp and presence lifting me up?
44. What component of my relationship with the Lord makes me the most thankful?
45. Which Bible scripture is my favorite, and why?
46. Do I just celebrate when things are going well? Can I celebrate while in famine?
47. What transgressions must I repent of to the Lord?
48. Make a list of song lyrics that speak to me and explain why.
49. What has been the greatest blessing so far in my life?
50. What am I sensing God calling me to change in my life?

November

"Some will tell you that there are multiple worldviews. The Bible says we have only two: the Truth and the Lie."
—Mark Driscoll

November

1. _____
2. _____
3. _____
4. _____
5. _____
6. _____
7. _____
8. _____
9. _____
10. _____
11. _____
12. _____
13. _____
14. _____
15. _____
16. _____
17. _____
18. _____
19. _____
20. _____
21. _____
22. _____
23. _____
24. _____
25. _____
26. _____
27. _____
28. _____
29. _____
30. _____

Monthly Intention	Monthly Reflection
This month's prayer focus:	What I'm thankful for this month:
To make this month great I will:	What I have learned about God:
What I'm looking forward to this month:	Who I served this month:

Weekly Bible Goals/Faith In Action

Date: _____

Sunday	
Monday	
Tuesday	
Wednesday	
Thursday	
Friday	
Saturday	

IT'S ALL ABOUT JESUS

Weekly Reflection

Before I Start My Week:	After My Week Ends:
What am I grateful for?	How did I see God working in me?
What does God want me to do this week?	Was I honoring God with my actions?
What area do I want God to bless me?	What things could I have done differently?
How can I be Salt & Light to my community?	How did I reflect Christ's love this week?

Scripture Studied

Author:_____   Where:_____

When:_____   Why:_____

Scripture:

Cross Reverences::

Observation:

Application:

Notes:

IT'S ALL ABOUT JESUS

Summary of What I Learned

Important Locations:

Memory Verse

Key Words:

Questions:

Key People:

IT'S ALL ABOUT JESUS

Weekly Prayer

My Prayer Focus:

My praise and worship

Lord I am grateful for...

Lord teach me to....

What are the struggles I am facing?

What may be God's answer to my prayer?

Prayer:

IT'S ALL ABOUT JESUS

Weekly Revelation

How did the Lord speak to me?
_____
_____
_____
_____

Discription of what I saw/heard:

How do I feel about this revelation?
_____
_____
_____
_____

What may be the interpretation?
_____
_____
_____
_____
_____
_____
_____
_____

Biblical References:
- _____
- _____
- _____
- _____
- _____

IT'S ALL ABOUT JESUS

Weekly Self-Reflection

Verse:_____   Topic:_____

What's the context?
_____
_____
_____

Similar Verses:
- _____
- _____
- _____
- _____
- _____
- _____

My initial thoughts:
_____
_____
_____

What immediately stands out to me about this verse?
_____
_____
_____
_____

Does this show me how Christians are supposed to live?
_____
_____
_____
_____

Is there an example of this verse in the first 5 books of the Bible?
_____
_____
_____
_____

Does this remind me of anything Jesus said or did?
_____
_____
_____
_____

IT'S ALL ABOUT JESUS

Weekly Self-Reflection

Question I am pondering about today:

Self-Reflection Journal Prompts

1. What is God asking me to prioritize over the upcoming six months?
2. Today, God has given me someone to pray for.
3. Is my behavior this week indicating that I'm content with my life circumstances?
4. Who is God urging me to let go of my grudge against?
5. What aspects of the fruit of the Spirit do I need to enlist assistance in developing?
6. How can I help others by shining a light in a dark place?
7. Is there a time when I feel the most distant from the Lord?
8. How is my arrogance driving me to cause harm to others?
9. Do I find it difficult to communicate my regrets? If that's the case, why?
10. Choose a Biblical figure. What can I glean from their narrative?
11. What or who do I fear? Why?
12. How does God want me to listen to him?
13. What is the "next step" for my spiritual growth?
14. Am I pleasing God in my singleness/ married life/ as a parent?
15. Is there anything in my life that I should put my trust in the Lord for?
16. Describe the three most vulnerable areas of myself.
17. Describe three occasions in my life when the Lord provided for me and served as my protection.
18. According to Ecclesiastes, there is a season for everything. Which season am I now in?
19. Write my own Psalm of praise/thanksgiving to God.
20. When did Jesus Christ become my Lord and Savior?
21. How might I live within the anointing of the Lord?
22. Recall a period in my life when the Lord delivered me.
23. In my perspective, what will heaven be like?
24. What might I do this year to improve my patience?
25. How could I become more grateful this year?
26. Is it possible that I'm growing arrogant in some way? How can I make it right?
27. How can I make this year more enjoyable?
28. How can I make this year a more peaceful one for myself?
29. What could I do this year to cultivate obedience to the Lord?
30. How can I love more this year?
31. How can I become nicer and gentler this year?
32. Write a letter of forgiveness to an enemy.
33. If I am struggling with something, what do I think God wants me to learn from it?
34. What spiritual gifts do I possess? What can I do with them to further God's kingdom?
35. Write on a time when the Lord spoke to me.
36. Be still and listen. What is the Lord revealing to me at this moment?
37. When do I most strongly feel God's presence? What can I do when I don't feel His presence near?
38. The last time something angered me, how did I react to it? What does the reply reveal about my character?
39. How does my pride respond when something offends me?
40. How can I experience the Lord's healing in my life?
41. Who is one individual I can specifically help? How?
42. What steals my peace by diverting my thoughts from God?
43. When have I sensed God's grasp and presence lifting me up?
44. What component of my relationship with the Lord makes me the most thankful?
45. Which Bible scripture is my favorite, and why?
46. Do I just celebrate when things are going well? Can I celebrate while in famine?
47. What transgressions must I repent of to the Lord?
48. Make a list of song lyrics that speak to me and explain why.
49. What has been the greatest blessing so far in my life?
50. What am I sensing God calling me to change in my life?

IT'S ALL ABOUT JESUS

Weekly Bible Goals/Faith In Action

Date: _____

Day	
Sunday	
Monday	
Tuesday	
Wednesday	
Thursday	
Friday	
Saturday	

Weekly Reflection

Before I Start My Week:

What am I grateful for?

What does God want me to do this week?

What area do I want God to bless me?

How can I be Salt & Light to my community?

After My Week Ends:

How did I see God working in me?

Was I honoring God with my actions?

What things could I have done differently?

How did I reflect Christ's love this week?

IT'S ALL ABOUT JESUS

Scripture Studied

Author:_____   Where:_____

When:_____   Why:_____

Scripture:

_____
_____
_____
_____
_____
_____

Cross Reverences::

_____
_____
_____
_____

Observation:

Application:

Notes:

_____
_____
_____
_____
_____

Summary of What I Learned

Important Locations:

Memory Verse

Key Words:

Questions:

Key People:

IT'S ALL ABOUT JESUS

Weekly Prayer

My Prayer Focus:

My praise and worship
_____
_____
_____
_____

Lord I am grateful for...
_____
_____
_____
_____

Lord teach me to....
_____
_____
_____
_____

What are the struggles I am facing?
_____
_____
_____
_____

What may be God's answer to my prayer?
_____
_____
_____
_____

Prayer:
_____
_____
_____
_____
_____
_____
_____
_____
_____
_____
_____
_____
_____
_____
_____
_____
_____
_____
_____
_____
_____
_____

Weekly Revelation

How did the Lord speak to me?
_____
_____
_____
_____
_____

Discription of what I saw/heard:

How do I feel about this revelation?
_____
_____
_____
_____
_____
_____
_____

What may be the interpretation?
_____
_____
_____
_____
_____
_____
_____
_____
_____
_____
_____

Biblical References:
- _____
- _____
- _____
- _____
- _____

IT'S ALL ABOUT JESUS

Weekly Self-Reflection

Verse:_____   Topic:_____

What's the context?
_____
_____
_____

Similar Verses:
- _____
- _____
- _____
- _____
- _____
- _____

My initial thoughts:
_____
_____
_____

What immediately stands out to me about this verse?
_____
_____
_____
_____

Does this show me how Christians are supposed to live?
_____
_____
_____
_____

Is there an example of this verse in the first 5 books of the Bible?
_____
_____
_____
_____

Does this remind me of anything Jesus said or did?
_____
_____
_____
_____

Weekly Self-Reflection

Question I am pondering about today:

IT'S ALL ABOUT JESUS

Self-Reflection Journal Prompts

1. What is God asking me to prioritize over the upcoming six months?
2. Today, God has given me someone to pray for.
3. Is my behavior this week indicating that I'm content with my life circumstances?
4. Who is God urging me to let go of my grudge against?
5. What aspects of the fruit of the Spirit do I need to enlist assistance in developing?
6. How can I help others by shining a light in a dark place?
7. Is there a time when I feel the most distant from the Lord?
8. How is my arrogance driving me to cause harm to others?
9. Do I find it difficult to communicate my regrets? If that's the case, why?
10. Choose a Biblical figure. What can I glean from their narrative?
11. What or who do I fear? Why?
12. How does God want me to listen to him?
13. What is the "next step" for my spiritual growth?
14. Am I pleasing God in my singleness/ married life/ as a parent?
15. Is there anything in my life that I should put my trust in the Lord for?
16. Describe the three most vulnerable areas of myself.
17. Describe three occasions in my life when the Lord provided for me and served as my protection.
18. According to Ecclesiastes, there is a season for everything. Which season am I now in?
19. Write my own Psalm of praise/thanksgiving to God.
20. When did Jesus Christ become my Lord and Savior?
21. How might I live within the anointing of the Lord?
22. Recall a period in my life when the Lord delivered me.
23. In my perspective, what will heaven be like?
24. What might I do this year to improve my patience?
25. How could I become more grateful this year?
26. Is it possible that I'm growing arrogant in some way? How can I make it right?
27. How can I make this year more enjoyable?
28. How can I make this year a more peaceful one for myself?
29. What could I do this year to cultivate obedience to the Lord?
30. How can I love more this year?
31. How can I become nicer and gentler this year?
32. Write a letter of forgiveness to an enemy.
33. If I am struggling with something, what do I think God wants me to learn from it?
34. What spiritual gifts do I possess? What can I do with them to further God's kingdom?
35. Write on a time when the Lord spoke to me.
36. Be still and listen. What is the Lord revealing to me at this moment?
37. When do I most strongly feel God's presence? What can I do when I don't feel His presence near?
38. The last time something angered me, how did I react to it? What does the reply reveal about my character?
39. How does my pride respond when something offends me?
40. How can I experience the Lord's healing in my life?
41. Who is one individual I can specifically help? How?
42. What steals my peace by diverting my thoughts from God?
43. When have I sensed God's grasp and presence lifting me up?
44. What component of my relationship with the Lord makes me the most thankful?
45. Which Bible scripture is my favorite, and why?
46. Do I just celebrate when things are going well? Can I celebrate while in famine?
47. What transgressions must I repent of to the Lord?
48. Make a list of song lyrics that speak to me and explain why.
49. What has been the greatest blessing so far in my life?
50. What am I sensing God calling me to change in my life?

Weekly Bible Goals/Faith In Action

Date: _____

Sunday	
Monday	
Tuesday	
Wednesday	
Thursday	
Friday	
Saturday	

IT'S ALL ABOUT JESUS

Weekly Reflection

Before I Start My Week:	After My Week Ends:
What am I grateful for?	How did I see God working in me?
What does God want me to do this week?	Was I honoring God with my actions?
What area do I want God to bless me?	What things could I have done differently?
How can I be Salt & Light to my community?	How did I reflect Christ's love this week?

Scripture Studied

Author:_____ Where:_____

When:_____ Why:_____

Scripture:

Cross Reverences::

Observation:

Application:

Notes:
_____
_____
_____
_____
_____

IT'S ALL ABOUT JESUS

Summary of What I Learned

Important Locations:

Memory Verse

Key Words:

Key People:

Questions:

Weekly Prayer

My Prayer Focus:

My praise and worship

_____
_____
_____

Lord I am grateful for...

_____
_____
_____
_____

Lord teach me to....

_____
_____
_____
_____

What are the struggles I am facing?

_____
_____
_____
_____

What may be God's answer to my prayer?

_____
_____
_____
_____

Prayer:

_____
_____
_____
_____
_____
_____
_____
_____
_____
_____
_____
_____
_____
_____
_____
_____
_____
_____
_____
_____
_____
_____
_____
_____
_____
_____
_____

IT'S ALL ABOUT JESUS

Weekly Revelation

How did the Lord speak to me?
_____
_____
_____
_____

Discription of what I saw/heard:

How do I feel about this revelation?
_____
_____
_____
_____
_____

What may be the interpretation?
_____
_____
_____
_____
_____
_____
_____
_____
_____

Biblical References :
- _____
- _____
- _____
- _____
- _____

IT'S ALL ABOUT JESUS

Weekly Self-Reflection

Verse:_____   Topic:_____

What's the context?
_____
_____
_____
_____

Similar Verses:
- _____
- _____
- _____
- _____
- _____
- _____

My initial thoughts:
_____
_____
_____
_____

What immediately stands out to me about this verse?
_____
_____
_____
_____
_____

Does this show me how Christians are supposed to live?
_____
_____
_____
_____
_____

Is there an example of this verse in the first 5 books of the Bible?
_____
_____
_____
_____
_____

Does this remind me of anything Jesus said or did?
_____
_____
_____
_____
_____

IT'S ALL ABOUT JESUS

Weekly Self-Reflection

Question I am pondering about today:

Self-Reflection Journal Prompts

1. What is God asking me to prioritize over the upcoming six months?
2. Today, God has given me someone to pray for.
3. Is my behavior this week indicating that I'm content with my life circumstances?
4. Who is God urging me to let go of my grudge against?
5. What aspects of the fruit of the Spirit do I need to enlist assistance in developing?
6. How can I help others by shining a light in a dark place?
7. Is there a time when I feel the most distant from the Lord?
8. How is my arrogance driving me to cause harm to others?
9. Do I find it difficult to communicate my regrets? If that's the case, why?
10. Choose a Biblical figure. What can I glean from their narrative?
11. What or who do I fear? Why?
12. How does God want me to listen to him?
13. What is the "next step" for my spiritual growth?
14. Am I pleasing God in my singleness/ married life/ as a parent?
15. Is there anything in my life that I should put my trust in the Lord for?
16. Describe the three most vulnerable areas of myself.
17. Describe three occasions in my life when the Lord provided for me and served as my protection.
18. According to Ecclesiastes, there is a season for everything. Which season am I now in?
19. Write my own Psalm of praise/thanksgiving to God.
20. When did Jesus Christ become my Lord and Savior?
21. How might I live within the anointing of the Lord?
22. Recall a period in my life when the Lord delivered me.
23. In my perspective, what will heaven be like?
24. What might I do this year to improve my patience?
25. How could I become more grateful this year?
26. Is it possible that I'm growing arrogant in some way? How can I make it right?
27. How can I make this year more enjoyable?
28. How can I make this year a more peaceful one for myself?
29. What could I do this year to cultivate obedience to the Lord?
30. How can I love more this year?
31. How can I become nicer and gentler this year?
32. Write a letter of forgiveness to an enemy.
33. If I am struggling with something, what do I think God wants me to learn from it?
34. What spiritual gifts do I possess? What can I do with them to further God's kingdom?
35. Write on a time when the Lord spoke to me.
36. Be still and listen. What is the Lord revealing to me at this moment?
37. When do I most strongly feel God's presence? What can I do when I don't feel His presence near?
38. The last time something angered me, how did I react to it? What does the reply reveal about my character?
39. How does my pride respond when something offends me?
40. How can I experience the Lord's healing in my life?
41. Who is one individual I can specifically help? How?
42. What steals my peace by diverting my thoughts from God?
43. When have I sensed God's grasp and presence lifting me up?
44. What component of my relationship with the Lord makes me the most thankful?
45. Which Bible scripture is my favorite, and why?
46. Do I just celebrate when things are going well? Can I celebrate while in famine?
47. What transgressions must I repent of to the Lord?
48. Make a list of song lyrics that speak to me and explain why.
49. What has been the greatest blessing so far in my life?
50. What am I sensing God calling me to change in my life?

IT'S ALL ABOUT JESUS

Weekly Bible Goals/Faith In Action

Date: _____

Sunday	
Monday	
Tuesday	
Wednesday	
Thursday	
Friday	
Saturday	

IT'S ALL ABOUT JESUS

Weekly Reflection

Before I Start My Week:	After My Week Ends:
What am I grateful for?	How did I see God working in me?
What does God want me to do this week?	Was I honoring God with my actions?
What area do I want God to bless me?	What things could I have done differently?
How can I be Salt & Light to my community?	How did I reflect Christ's love this week?

IT'S ALL ABOUT JESUS

Scripture Studied

Author:_____ Where:_____

When:_____ Why:_____

Scripture:

Cross Reverences::

Observation:

Application:

Notes:

Summary of What I Learned

Important Locations:

Memory Verse

Key Words:

Questions:

Key People:

IT'S ALL ABOUT JESUS

Weekly Prayer

My Prayer Focus:

My praise and worship

Lord I am grateful for...

Lord teach me to....

What are the struggles I am facing?

What may be God's answer to my prayer?

Prayer:

Weekly Revelation

How did the Lord speak to me?

_____
_____
_____
_____

Discription of what I saw/heard:

How do I feel about this revelation?

_____
_____
_____
_____
_____

What may be the interpretation?

_____
_____
_____
_____
_____
_____
_____
_____

Biblical References :

- _____
- _____
- _____
- _____
- _____

IT'S ALL ABOUT JESUS

Weekly Self-Reflection

Verse:_____   Topic:_____

What's the context?

Similar Verses :

- _____
- _____
- _____
- _____
- _____
- _____

My initial thoughts:

What immediately stands out to me about this verse?

Does this show me how Christians are supposed to live?

Is there an example of this verse in the first 5 books of the Bible?

Does this remind me of anything Jesus said or did?

Weekly Self-Reflection

Question I am pondering about today:

IT'S ALL ABOUT JESUS

Self-Reflection Journal Prompts

1. What is God asking me to prioritize over the upcoming six months?
2. Today, God has given me someone to pray for.
3. Is my behavior this week indicating that I'm content with my life circumstances?
4. Who is God urging me to let go of my grudge against?
5. What aspects of the fruit of the Spirit do I need to enlist assistance in developing?
6. How can I help others by shining a light in a dark place?
7. Is there a time when I feel the most distant from the Lord?
8. How is my arrogance driving me to cause harm to others?
9. Do I find it difficult to communicate my regrets? If that's the case, why?
10. Choose a Biblical figure. What can I glean from their narrative?
11. What or who do I fear? Why?
12. How does God want me to listen to him?
13. What is the "next step" for my spiritual growth?
14. Am I pleasing God in my singleness/ married life/ as a parent?
15. Is there anything in my life that I should put my trust in the Lord for?
16. Describe the three most vulnerable areas of myself.
17. Describe three occasions in my life when the Lord provided for me and served as my protection.
18. According to Ecclesiastes, there is a season for everything. Which season am I now in?
19. Write my own Psalm of praise/thanksgiving to God.
20. When did Jesus Christ become my Lord and Savior?
21. How might I live within the anointing of the Lord?
22. Recall a period in my life when the Lord delivered me.
23. In my perspective, what will heaven be like?
24. What might I do this year to improve my patience?
25. How could I become more grateful this year?
26. Is it possible that I'm growing arrogant in some way? How can I make it right?
27. How can I make this year more enjoyable?
28. How can I make this year a more peaceful one for myself?
29. What could I do this year to cultivate obedience to the Lord?
30. How can I love more this year?
31. How can I become nicer and gentler this year?
32. Write a letter of forgiveness to an enemy.
33. If I am struggling with something, what do I think God wants me to learn from it?
34. What spiritual gifts do I possess? What can I do with them to further God's kingdom?
35. Write on a time when the Lord spoke to me.
36. Be still and listen. What is the Lord revealing to me at this moment?
37. When do I most strongly feel God's presence? What can I do when I don't feel His presence near?
38. The last time something angered me, how did I react to it? What does the reply reveal about my character?
39. How does my pride respond when something offends me?
40. How can I experience the Lord's healing in my life?
41. Who is one individual I can specifically help? How?
42. What steals my peace by diverting my thoughts from God?
43. When have I sensed God's grasp and presence lifting me up?
44. What component of my relationship with the Lord makes me the most thankful?
45. Which Bible scripture is my favorite, and why?
46. Do I just celebrate when things are going well? Can I celebrate while in famine?
47. What transgressions must I repent of to the Lord?
48. Make a list of song lyrics that speak to me and explain why.
49. What has been the greatest blessing so far in my life?
50. What am I sensing God calling me to change in my life?

December

"Ultimately I think the difference between reading the Bible and studying it is making the connections between who Jesus is and what he's done."
—Mark Driscoll

December

1. _____
2. _____
3. _____
4. _____
5. _____
6. _____
7. _____
8. _____
9. _____
10. _____
11. _____
12. _____
13. _____
14. _____
15. _____
16. _____
17. _____
18. _____
19. _____
20. _____
21. _____
22. _____
23. _____
24. _____
25. _____
26. _____
27. _____
28. _____
29. _____
30. _____
31. _____

Monthly Intention	Monthly Reflection
This month's prayer focus:	What I'm thankful for this month:
To make this month great I will:	What I have learned about God:
What I'm looking forward to this month:	Who I served this month:

Weekly Bible Goals/Faith In Action

Date: _____

Sunday	
Monday	
Tuesday	
Wednesday	
Thursday	
Friday	
Saturday	

IT'S ALL ABOUT JESUS

Weekly Reflection

Before I Start My Week:	After My Week Ends:
What am I grateful for?	How did I see God working in me?
What does God want me to do this week?	Was I honoring God with my actions?
What area do I want God to bless me?	What things could I have done differently?
How can I be Salt & Light to my community?	How did I reflect Christ's love this week?

Scripture Studied

Author:_____ Where:_____

When:_____ Why:_____

Scripture:

Cross Reverences::

Observation:

Application:

Notes:

IT'S ALL ABOUT JESUS

Summary of What I Learned

Important Locations:

Memory Verse

Key Words:

Questions:

Key People:

Weekly Prayer

My Prayer Focus:

My praise and worship

_____
_____
_____
_____

Lord I am grateful for...

_____
_____
_____
_____

Lord teach me to....

_____
_____
_____
_____

What are the struggles I am facing?

_____
_____
_____
_____

What may be God's answer to my prayer?

_____
_____
_____
_____

Prayer:

_____
_____
_____
_____
_____
_____
_____
_____
_____
_____
_____
_____
_____
_____
_____
_____
_____
_____
_____
_____

IT'S ALL ABOUT JESUS

Weekly Revelation

How did the Lord speak to me?
_____
_____
_____
_____
_____

Discription of what I saw/heard:

How do I feel about this revelation?
_____
_____
_____
_____
_____

What may be the interpretation?
_____
_____
_____
_____
_____
_____
_____
_____
_____

Biblical References :
- _____
- _____
- _____
- _____
- _____

IT'S ALL ABOUT JESUS

Weekly Self-Reflection

Verse:_____   Topic:_____

What's the context?
_____
_____
_____
_____

Similar Verses:
- _____
- _____
- _____
- _____
- _____
- _____

My initial thoughts:
_____
_____
_____
_____

What immediately stands out to me about this verse?
_____
_____
_____
_____
_____

Does this show me how Christians are supposed to live?
_____
_____
_____
_____
_____

Is there an example of this verse in the first 5 books of the Bible?
_____
_____
_____
_____

Does this remind me of anything Jesus said or did?
_____
_____
_____
_____
_____

IT'S ALL ABOUT JESUS

Weekly Self-Reflection

Question I am pondering about today:

Self-Reflection Journal Prompts

1. What is God asking me to prioritize over the upcoming six months?
2. Today, God has given me someone to pray for.
3. Is my behavior this week indicating that I'm content with my life circumstances?
4. Who is God urging me to let go of my grudge against?
5. What aspects of the fruit of the Spirit do I need to enlist assistance in developing?
6. How can I help others by shining a light in a dark place?
7. Is there a time when I feel the most distant from the Lord?
8. How is my arrogance driving me to cause harm to others?
9. Do I find it difficult to communicate my regrets? If that's the case, why?
10. Choose a Biblical figure. What can I glean from their narrative?
11. What or who do I fear? Why?
12. How does God want me to listen to him?
13. What is the "next step" for my spiritual growth?
14. Am I pleasing God in my singleness/ married life/ as a parent?
15. Is there anything in my life that I should put my trust in the Lord for?
16. Describe the three most vulnerable areas of myself.
17. Describe three occasions in my life when the Lord provided for me and served as my protection.
18. According to Ecclesiastes, there is a season for everything. Which season am I now in?
19. Write my own Psalm of praise/thanksgiving to God.
20. When did Jesus Christ become my Lord and Savior?
21. How might I live within the anointing of the Lord?
22. Recall a period in my life when the Lord delivered me.
23. In my perspective, what will heaven be like?
24. What might I do this year to improve my patience?
25. How could I become more grateful this year?
26. Is it possible that I'm growing arrogant in some way? How can I make it right?
27. How can I make this year more enjoyable?
28. How can I make this year a more peaceful one for myself?
29. What could I do this year to cultivate obedience to the Lord?
30. How can I love more this year?
31. How can I become nicer and gentler this year?
32. Write a letter of forgiveness to an enemy.
33. If I am struggling with something, what do I think God wants me to learn from it?
34. What spiritual gifts do I possess? What can I do with them to further God's kingdom?
35. Write on a time when the Lord spoke to me.
36. Be still and listen. What is the Lord revealing to me at this moment?
37. When do I most strongly feel God's presence? What can I do when I don't feel His presence near?
38. The last time something angered me, how did I react to it? What does the reply reveal about my character?
39. How does my pride respond when something offends me?
40. How can I experience the Lord's healing in my life?
41. Who is one individual I can specifically help? How?
42. What steals my peace by diverting my thoughts from God?
43. When have I sensed God's grasp and presence lifting me up?
44. What component of my relationship with the Lord makes me the most thankful?
45. Which Bible scripture is my favorite, and why?
46. Do I just celebrate when things are going well? Can I celebrate while in famine?
47. What transgressions must I repent of to the Lord?
48. Make a list of song lyrics that speak to me and explain why.
49. What has been the greatest blessing so far in my life?
50. What am I sensing God calling me to change in my life?

IT'S ALL ABOUT JESUS

Weekly Bible Goals/Faith In Action

Date: _____

Day	
Sunday	
Monday	
Tuesday	
Wednesday	
Thursday	
Friday	
Saturday	

Weekly Reflection

Before I Start My Week:

What am I grateful for?

What does God want me to do this week?

What area do I want God to bless me?

How can I be Salt & Light to my community?

After My Week Ends:

How did I see God working in me?

Was I honoring God with my actions?

What things could I have done differently?

How did I reflect Christ's love this week?

IT'S ALL ABOUT JESUS

Scripture Studied

Author:_____ Where:_____

When:_____ Why:_____

Scripture:

Cross Reverences::

Observation:

Application:

Notes:

Summary of What I Learned

_____
_____
_____
_____
_____
_____

Important Locations:

Memory Verse

Key Words:
- _____
- _____
- _____
- _____
- _____

Questions:
- _____
- _____
- _____
- _____
- _____

Key People:
- _____
- _____
- _____
- _____

IT'S ALL ABOUT JESUS

Weekly Prayer

My Prayer Focus:

_____
_____
_____

My praise and worship	Prayer:

My praise and worship
_____
_____
_____
_____

Lord I am grateful for...
_____
_____
_____
_____

Lord teach me to....
_____
_____
_____
_____

What are the struggles I am facing?
_____
_____
_____
_____

What may be God's answer to my prayer?
_____
_____
_____
_____

Weekly Revelation

How did the Lord speak to me?
_____
_____
_____
_____
_____

Discription of what I saw/heard:

How do I feel about this revelation?
_____
_____
_____
_____
_____
_____

What may be the interpretation?
_____
_____
_____
_____
_____
_____
_____
_____
_____
_____

Biblical References :
- _____
- _____
- _____
- _____
- _____

IT'S ALL ABOUT JESUS

Weekly Self-Reflection

Verse:_____   Topic:_____

What's the context?   Similar Verses:
_____   • _____
_____
_____   • _____

My initial thoughts: • _____
_____
_____   • _____
_____
                                           • _____

                                           • _____

What immediately stands out to me about this verse?
_____
_____
_____
_____

Does this show me how Christians are supposed to live?
_____
_____
_____
_____

Is there an example of this verse in the first 5 books of the Bible?
_____
_____
_____
_____

Does this remind me of anything Jesus said or did?
_____
_____
_____
_____

Weekly Self-Reflection

Question I am pondering about today:

IT'S ALL ABOUT JESUS

Self-Reflection Journal Prompts

1. What is God asking me to prioritize over the upcoming six months?
2. Today, God has given me someone to pray for.
3. Is my behavior this week indicating that I'm content with my life circumstances?
4. Who is God urging me to let go of my grudge against?
5. What aspects of the fruit of the Spirit do I need to enlist assistance in developing?
6. How can I help others by shining a light in a dark place?
7. Is there a time when I feel the most distant from the Lord?
8. How is my arrogance driving me to cause harm to others?
9. Do I find it difficult to communicate my regrets? If that's the case, why?
10. Choose a Biblical figure. What can I glean from their narrative?
11. What or who do I fear? Why?
12. How does God want me to listen to him?
13. What is the "next step" for my spiritual growth?
14. Am I pleasing God in my singleness/ married life/ as a parent?
15. Is there anything in my life that I should put my trust in the Lord for?
16. Describe the three most vulnerable areas of myself.
17. Describe three occasions in my life when the Lord provided for me and served as my protection.
18. According to Ecclesiastes, there is a season for everything. Which season am I now in?
19. Write my own Psalm of praise/thanksgiving to God.
20. When did Jesus Christ become my Lord and Savior?
21. How might I live within the anointing of the Lord?
22. Recall a period in my life when the Lord delivered me.
23. In my perspective, what will heaven be like?
24. What might I do this year to improve my patience?
25. How could I become more grateful this year?
26. Is it possible that I'm growing arrogant in some way? How can I make it right?
27. How can I make this year more enjoyable?
28. How can I make this year a more peaceful one for myself?
29. What could I do this year to cultivate obedience to the Lord?
30. How can I love more this year?
31. How can I become nicer and gentler this year?
32. Write a letter of forgiveness to an enemy.
33. If I am struggling with something, what do I think God wants me to learn from it?
34. What spiritual gifts do I possess? What can I do with them to further God's kingdom?
35. Write on a time when the Lord spoke to me.
36. Be still and listen. What is the Lord revealing to me at this moment?
37. When do I most strongly feel God's presence? What can I do when I don't feel His presence near?
38. The last time something angered me, how did I react to it? What does the reply reveal about my character?
39. How does my pride respond when something offends me?
40. How can I experience the Lord's healing in my life?
41. Who is one individual I can specifically help? How?
42. What steals my peace by diverting my thoughts from God?
43. When have I sensed God's grasp and presence lifting me up?
44. What component of my relationship with the Lord makes me the most thankful?
45. Which Bible scripture is my favorite, and why?
46. Do I just celebrate when things are going well? Can I celebrate while in famine?
47. What transgressions must I repent of to the Lord?
48. Make a list of song lyrics that speak to me and explain why.
49. What has been the greatest blessing so far in my life?
50. What am I sensing God calling me to change in my life?

Weekly Bible Goals/Faith In Action

Date: _____

Sunday	
Monday	
Tuesday	
Wednesday	
Thursday	
Friday	
Saturday	

IT'S ALL ABOUT JESUS

Weekly Reflection

Before I Start My Week:

What am I grateful for?

What does God want me to do this week?

What area do I want God to bless me?

How can I be Salt & Light to my community?

After My Week Ends:

How did I see God working in me?

Was I honoring God with my actions?

What things could I have done differently?

How did I reflect Christ's love this week?

Scripture Studied

Author:_____   Where:_____

When:_____   Why:_____

Scripture:

Cross Reverences::

Observation:

Application:

Notes:
_____
_____
_____
_____
_____

IT'S ALL ABOUT JESUS

Summary of What I Learned

Important Locations:

Memory Verse

Key Words:
- _____
- _____
- _____
- _____
- _____

Questions:
- _____
- _____
- _____
- _____
- _____
- _____

Key People:
- _____
- _____
- _____
- _____

Weekly Prayer

My Prayer Focus:

My praise and worship

_____
_____
_____
_____

Lord I am grateful for...

_____
_____
_____
_____

Lord teach me to....

_____
_____
_____
_____

What are the struggles I am facing?

_____
_____
_____
_____

What may be God's answer to my prayer?

_____
_____
_____
_____

Prayer:

_____
_____
_____
_____
_____
_____
_____
_____
_____
_____
_____
_____
_____
_____
_____
_____
_____
_____
_____
_____
_____
_____
_____
_____

IT'S ALL ABOUT JESUS

Weekly Revelation

How did the Lord speak to me?

_____
_____
_____
_____

Discription of what I saw/heard:

How do I feel about this revelation?

_____
_____
_____
_____
_____
_____

What may be the interpretation?

_____
_____
_____
_____
_____
_____
_____
_____
_____
_____

Biblical References :

- _____
- _____
- _____
- _____
- _____

Weekly Self-Reflection

Verse:_____   Topic:_____

What's the context?

_____
_____
_____

My initial thoughts:

_____
_____
_____

Similar Verses:

- _____
- _____
- _____
- _____
- _____
- _____

What immediately stands out to me about this verse?

_____
_____
_____
_____

Does this show me how Christians are supposed to live?

_____
_____
_____
_____

Is there an example of this verse in the first 5 books of the Bible?

_____
_____
_____
_____

Does this remind me of anything Jesus said or did?

_____
_____
_____
_____

IT'S ALL ABOUT JESUS

Weekly Self-Reflection

Question I am pondering about today:

Self-Reflection Journal Prompts

1. What is God asking me to prioritize over the upcoming six months?
2. Today, God has given me someone to pray for.
3. Is my behavior this week indicating that I'm content with my life circumstances?
4. Who is God urging me to let go of my grudge against?
5. What aspects of the fruit of the Spirit do I need to enlist assistance in developing?
6. How can I help others by shining a light in a dark place?
7. Is there a time when I feel the most distant from the Lord?
8. How is my arrogance driving me to cause harm to others?
9. Do I find it difficult to communicate my regrets? If that's the case, why?
10. Choose a Biblical figure. What can I glean from their narrative?
11. What or who do I fear? Why?
12. How does God want me to listen to him?
13. What is the "next step" for my spiritual growth?
14. Am I pleasing God in my singleness/ married life/ as a parent?
15. Is there anything in my life that I should put my trust in the Lord for?
16. Describe the three most vulnerable areas of myself.
17. Describe three occasions in my life when the Lord provided for me and served as my protection.
18. According to Ecclesiastes, there is a season for everything. Which season am I now in?
19. Write my own Psalm of praise/thanksgiving to God.
20. When did Jesus Christ become my Lord and Savior?
21. How might I live within the anointing of the Lord?
22. Recall a period in my life when the Lord delivered me.
23. In my perspective, what will heaven be like?
24. What might I do this year to improve my patience?
25. How could I become more grateful this year?
26. Is it possible that I'm growing arrogant in some way? How can I make it right?
27. How can I make this year more enjoyable?
28. How can I make this year a more peaceful one for myself?
29. What could I do this year to cultivate obedience to the Lord?
30. How can I love more this year?
31. How can I become nicer and gentler this year?
32. Write a letter of forgiveness to an enemy.
33. If I am struggling with something, what do I think God wants me to learn from it?
34. What spiritual gifts do I possess? What can I do with them to further God's kingdom?
35. Write on a time when the Lord spoke to me.
36. Be still and listen. What is the Lord revealing to me at this moment?
37. When do I most strongly feel God's presence? What can I do when I don't feel His presence near?
38. The last time something angered me, how did I react to it? What does the reply reveal about my character?
39. How does my pride respond when something offends me?
40. How can I experience the Lord's healing in my life?
41. Who is one individual I can specifically help? How?
42. What steals my peace by diverting my thoughts from God?
43. When have I sensed God's grasp and presence lifting me up?
44. What component of my relationship with the Lord makes me the most thankful?
45. Which Bible scripture is my favorite, and why?
46. Do I just celebrate when things are going well? Can I celebrate while in famine?
47. What transgressions must I repent of to the Lord?
48. Make a list of song lyrics that speak to me and explain why.
49. What has been the greatest blessing so far in my life?
50. What am I sensing God calling me to change in my life?

IT'S ALL ABOUT JESUS

Weekly Bible Goals/Faith In Action

Date: _____

Sunday	
Monday	
Tuesday	
Wednesday	
Thursday	
Friday	
Saturday	

Weekly Reflection

Before I Start My Week:

What am I grateful for?

What does God want me to do this week?

What area do I want God to bless me?

How can I be Salt & Light to my community?

After My Week Ends:

How did I see God working in me?

Was I honoring God with my actions?

What things could I have done differently?

How did I reflect Christ's love this week?

IT'S ALL ABOUT JESUS

Scripture Studied

Author:_____   Where:_____

When:_____   Why:_____

Scripture:

Cross Reverences::

Observation:

Application:

Notes:

Summary of What I Learned

_____
_____
_____
_____
_____

Important Locations:

Memory Verse
_____
_____
_____
_____
_____
_____
_____
_____
_____
_____
_____
_____
_____
_____
_____

Key Words:
- _____
- _____
- _____
- _____
- _____

Questions:
- _____
- _____
- _____
- _____
- _____

Key People:
- _____
- _____
- _____
- _____

IT'S ALL ABOUT JESUS

Weekly Prayer

My Prayer Focus:

My praise and worship

Lord I am grateful for...

Lord teach me to....

What are the struggles I am facing?

What may be God's answer to my prayer?

Prayer:

Weekly Revelation

How did the Lord speak to me?
_____
_____
_____
_____
_____

Discription of what I saw/heard:

How do I feel about this revelation?
_____
_____
_____
_____
_____
_____
_____

What may be the interpretation?
_____
_____
_____
_____
_____
_____
_____
_____
_____
_____

Biblical References :
- _____
- _____
- _____
- _____
- _____

IT'S ALL ABOUT JESUS

Weekly Self-Reflection

Verse:_____ Topic:_____

What's the context?

_____
_____
_____

My initial thoughts:

_____
_____
_____
_____

Similar Verses:

- _____
- _____
- _____
- _____
- _____
- _____

What immediately stands out to me about this verse?

_____
_____
_____
_____

Does this show me how Christians are supposed to live?

_____
_____
_____
_____
_____

Is there an example of this verse in the first 5 books of the Bible?

_____
_____
_____
_____

Does this remind me of anything Jesus said or did?

_____
_____
_____
_____

IT'S ALL ABOUT JESUS

Weekly Self-Reflection

Question I am pondering about today:

IT'S ALL ABOUT JESUS

Self-Reflection Journal Prompts

1. What is God asking me to prioritize over the upcoming six months?
2. Today, God has given me someone to pray for.
3. Is my behavior this week indicating that I'm content with my life circumstances?
4. Who is God urging me to let go of my grudge against?
5. What aspects of the fruit of the Spirit do I need to enlist assistance in developing?
6. How can I help others by shining a light in a dark place?
7. Is there a time when I feel the most distant from the Lord?
8. How is my arrogance driving me to cause harm to others?
9. Do I find it difficult to communicate my regrets? If that's the case, why?
10. Choose a Biblical figure. What can I glean from their narrative?
11. What or who do I fear? Why?
12. How does God want me to listen to him?
13. What is the "next step" for my spiritual growth?
14. Am I pleasing God in my singleness/ married life/ as a parent?
15. Is there anything in my life that I should put my trust in the Lord for?
16. Describe the three most vulnerable areas of myself.
17. Describe three occasions in my life when the Lord provided for me and served as my protection.
18. According to Ecclesiastes, there is a season for everything. Which season am I now in?
19. Write my own Psalm of praise/thanksgiving to God.
20. When did Jesus Christ become my Lord and Savior?
21. How might I live within the anointing of the Lord?
22. Recall a period in my life when the Lord delivered me.
23. In my perspective, what will heaven be like?
24. What might I do this year to improve my patience?
25. How could I become more grateful this year?
26. Is it possible that I'm growing arrogant in some way? How can I make it right?
27. How can I make this year more enjoyable?
28. How can I make this year a more peaceful one for myself?
29. What could I do this year to cultivate obedience to the Lord?
30. How can I love more this year?
31. How can I become nicer and gentler this year?
32. Write a letter of forgiveness to an enemy.
33. If I am struggling with something, what do I think God wants me to learn from it?
34. What spiritual gifts do I possess? What can I do with them to further God's kingdom?
35. Write on a time when the Lord spoke to me.
36. Be still and listen. What is the Lord revealing to me at this moment?
37. When do I most strongly feel God's presence? What can I do when I don't feel His presence near?
38. The last time something angered me, how did I react to it? What does the reply reveal about my character?
39. How does my pride respond when something offends me?
40. How can I experience the Lord's healing in my life?
41. Who is one individual I can specifically help? How?
42. What steals my peace by diverting my thoughts from God?
43. When have I sensed God's grasp and presence lifting me up?
44. What component of my relationship with the Lord makes me the most thankful?
45. Which Bible scripture is my favorite, and why?
46. Do I just celebrate when things are going well? Can I celebrate while in famine?
47. What transgressions must I repent of to the Lord?
48. Make a list of song lyrics that speak to me and explain why.
49. What has been the greatest blessing so far in my life?
50. What am I sensing God calling me to change in my life?

Topical Studies

Topical Study Log

Date	Topic	Key Scripture

Topical Study

Topic:

Notes:

Hebrew/Greek/Aramaic Definition:

Key Passages::

Key Phrases/Patterns:

What does this teach me about God?

Application:

IT'S ALL ABOUT JESUS

Topical Study

Topic:

Notes:

Hebrew/Greek/Aramaic Definition:

Key Passages::

Key Phrases/Patterns:

What does this teach me about God?

Application:

Topical Study

Topic:

Notes:

Hebrew/Greek/Aramaic Definition:

Key Passages:

Key Phrases/Patterns:

What does this teach me about God?

Application:

IT'S ALL ABOUT JESUS

Topical Study

Topic:

Notes:

Hebrew/Greek/Aramaic Definition:

Key Passages::

Key Phrases/Patterns:

What does this teach me about God?

Application:

Topical Study

Topic:

Notes:

Hebrew/Greek/Aramaic Definition:

Key Passages::

Key Phrases/Patterns:

What does this teach me about God?

Application:

IT'S ALL ABOUT JESUS

Topical Study

Topic:

Notes:

Hebrew/Greek/Aramaic Definition:

Key Passages::

Key Phrases/Patterns:

What does this teach me about God?

Application:

IT'S ALL ABOUT JESUS

Topical Study

Topic:

Notes:

Hebrew/Greek/Aramaic Definition:

Key Passages::

Key Phrases/Patterns:

What does this teach me about God?

Application:

IT'S ALL ABOUT JESUS

Topical Study

Topic:

Notes:

Hebrew/Greek/Aramaic Definition:

Key Passages::

Key Phrases/Patterns:

What does this teach me about God?

Application:

Topical Study

Topic:

Notes:

Hebrew/Greek/Aramaic Definition:

Key Passages::

Key Phrases/Patterns:

What does this teach me about God?

Application:

IT'S ALL ABOUT JESUS

Topical Study

Topic:

Notes:

Hebrew/Greek/Aramaic Definition:

Key Passages:

Key Phrases/Patterns:

What does this teach me about God?

Application:

Topical Study

Topic:

Notes:

Hebrew/Greek/Aramaic Definition:

Key Passages::

Key Phrases/Patterns:

What does this teach me about God?

Application:

IT'S ALL ABOUT JESUS

Topical Study

Topic:

Notes:

Hebrew/Greek/Aramaic Definition:

Key Passages::

Key Phrases/Patterns:

What does this teach me about God?

Application:

Chapter Studies

Chapter Study Log

Date	Book:Chapter	Key Scripture

Chapter Study

Passage:

Key words/phrases/patterns:
_____
_____
_____

Key people/places:
_____
_____
_____

What does this teach me about God?
_____
_____
_____
_____
_____
_____
_____

Main Lesson:
_____
_____
_____
_____
_____
_____

Key Verse
_____
_____
_____
_____
_____
_____

Chapter Outline/Notes:
_____
_____
_____
_____
_____
_____
_____
_____
_____
_____
_____
_____
_____
_____
_____
_____
_____
_____

IT'S ALL ABOUT JESUS

Chapter Study

Passage:

Key words/phrases/patterns:

Key Verse

Key people/places:

Chapter Outline/Notes:

What does this teach me about God?

Main Lesson:

It's All About Jesus

Chapter Study

Passage:

Key words/phrases/patterns:

Key people/places:

What does this teach me about God?

Main Lesson:

Key Verse

Chapter Outline/Notes:

IT'S ALL ABOUT JESUS

Chapter Study

Passage:

Key words/phrases/patterns:

Key people/places:

What does this teach me about God?

Main Lesson:

Key Verse

Chapter Outline/Notes:

Chapter Study

Passage:

Key words/phrases/patterns:

Key Verse

Key people/places:

Chapter Outline/Notes:

What does this teach me about God?

Main Lesson:

IT'S ALL ABOUT JESUS

Chapter Study

Passage:

Key words/phrases/patterns:

Key people/places:

What does this teach me about God?

Main Lesson:

Key Verse

Chapter Outline/Notes:

IT'S ALL ABOUT JESUS

Chapter Study

Passage:

Key words/phrases/patterns:

Key Verse

Key people/places:

Chapter Outline/Notes:

What does this teach me about God?

Main Lesson:

IT'S ALL ABOUT JESUS

Chapter Study

Passage:

Key words/phrases/patterns:

Key Verse

Key people/places:

Chapter Outline/Notes:

What does this teach me about God?

Main Lesson:

Chapter Study

Passage:

Key words/phrases/patterns:

Key people/places:

What does this teach me about God?

Main Lesson:

Key Verse

Chapter Outline/Notes:

IT'S ALL ABOUT JESUS

Chapter Study

Passage:

Key words/phrases/patterns:

Key people/places:

What does this teach me about God?

Main Lesson:

Key Verse

Chapter Outline/Notes:

IT'S ALL ABOUT JESUS

Chapter Study

Passage:

Key words/phrases/patterns:

Key Verse

Key people/places:

Chapter Outline/Notes:

What does this teach me about God?

Main Lesson:

IT'S ALL ABOUT JESUS

Chapter Study

Passage:

Key words/phrases/patterns:

Key people/places:

What does this teach me about God?

Main Lesson:

Key Verse

Chapter Outline/Notes:

IT'S ALL ABOUT JESUS

Verse Studies

Verse Mapping

Context

Who wrote it?

When?

Who to?

Why?

My Paraphrse

Another Translation

Word Study

Definition:

Hebrew/Greek/Aramaic Definition:

Other Ways This Verse is Translated:

Cross-References:

Verse

Notes:

Verse Reflection

Reflection

What does this teach me about the Lord?	What does this teach me about Mankind?

Personal Reflection

What is the Lord teaching me?	How can I apply this to my life?

IT'S ALL ABOUT JESUS

Verse Mapping

Context

Who wrote it?

When?

Who to?

Why?

My Paraphrse

Another Translation

Word Study

Definition:

Hebrew/Greek/Aramaic Definition:

Other Ways This Verse is Translated:

Cross-References:

Verse

Notes:

IT'S ALL ABOUT JESUS

Verse Reflection

Reflection

What does this teach me about the Lord?

What does this teach me about Mankind?

Personal Reflection

What is the Lord teaching me?

How can I apply this to my life?

IT'S ALL ABOUT JESUS

Verse Mapping

Context

Who wrote it?

When?

Who to?

Why?

My Paraphrse

Another Translation

Word Study

Definition:

Hebrew/Greek/Aramaic Definition:

Other Ways This Verse is Translated:

Cross-References:

Verse

Notes:

Verse Reflection

Reflection

What does this teach me about the Lord?

What does this teach me about Mankind?

Personal Reflection

What is the Lord teaching me?

How can I apply this to my life?

IT'S ALL ABOUT JESUS

Verse Mapping

Context

Who wrote it?
When?
Who to?
Why?

My Paraphrse

Another Translation

Word Study

Definition:

Hebrew/Greek/Aramaic Definition:

Other Ways This Verse is Translated:

Cross-References:

Verse

Notes:

Verse Reflection

Reflection

What does this teach me about the Lord?	What does this teach me about Mankind?

Personal Reflection

What is the Lord teaching me?	How can I apply this to my life?

IT'S ALL ABOUT JESUS

Verse Mapping

Context

Who wrote it?
_____
When?
_____
Who to?
_____
Why?
_____
_____

My Paraphrse

_____
_____
_____
_____
_____
_____
_____

Another Translation

_____
_____
_____
_____
_____
_____
_____

Word Study

Definition:
_____
_____
_____
_____

Hebrew/Greek/Aramaic Definition:
_____
_____
_____
_____

Other Ways This Verse is Translated:
_____
_____
_____
_____

Cross-References:
_____
_____
_____
_____

Verse

_____
_____
_____
_____
_____
_____

Notes:
_____
_____
_____
_____
_____
_____
_____
_____

IT'S ALL ABOUT JESUS

Verse Reflection

Reflection

What does this teach me about the Lord?	What does this teach me about Mankind?

Personal Reflection

What is the Lord teaching me?	How can I apply this to my life?

IT'S ALL ABOUT JESUS

Verse Mapping

Context

Who wrote it?

When?

Who to?

Why?

My Paraphrse

Another Translation

Word Study

Definition:

Hebrew/Greek/Aramaic Definition:

Other Ways This Verse is Translated:

Cross-References:

Verse

Notes:

Verse Reflection

Reflection

What does this teach me about the Lord?	What does this teach me about Mankind?

Personal Reflection

What is the Lord teaching me?	How can I apply this to my life?

IT'S ALL ABOUT JESUS

Verse Mapping

Context

Who wrote it?

When?

Who to?

Why?

My Paraphrse

Another Translation

Word Study

Definition:

Hebrew/Greek/Aramaic Definition:

Other Ways This Verse is Translated:

Cross-References:

Verse

Notes:

Verse Reflection

Reflection

What does this teach me about the Lord?	What does this teach me about Mankind?

Personal Reflection

What is the Lord teaching me?	How can I apply this to my life?

IT'S ALL ABOUT JESUS

Verse Mapping

Context

Who wrote it?
When?
Who to?
Why?

My Paraphrse

Another Translation

Word Study

Definition:

Hebrew/Greek/Aramaic Definition:

Other Ways This Verse is Translated:

Cross-References:

Verse

Notes:

Verse Reflection

Reflection

What does this teach me about the Lord?	What does this teach me about Mankind?

Personal Reflection

What is the Lord teaching me?	How can I apply this to my life?

IT'S ALL ABOUT JESUS

Verse Mapping

Context

Who wrote it?

When?

Who to?

Why?

My Paraphrse

Another Translation

Word Study

Definition:

Hebrew/Greek/Aramaic Definition:

Other Ways This Verse is Translated:

Cross-References:

Verse

Notes:

Verse Reflection

Reflection

What does this teach me about the Lord?

What does this teach me about Mankind?

Personal Reflection

What is the Lord teaching me?

How can I apply this to my life?

IT'S ALL ABOUT JESUS

Verse Mapping

Context

Who wrote it?

When?

Who to?

Why?

My Paraphrse

Another Translation

Word Study

Definition:

Hebrew/Greek/Aramaic Definition:

Other Ways This Verse is Translated:

Cross-References:

Verse

Notes:

Verse Reflection

Reflection

What does this teach me about the Lord?

What does this teach me about Mankind?

Personal Reflection

What is the Lord teaching me?

How can I apply this to my life?

IT'S ALL ABOUT JESUS

Verse Mapping

Context

Who wrote it?

When?

Who to?

Why?

My Paraphrse

Another Translation

Word Study

Definition:

Hebrew/Greek/Aramaic Definition:

Other Ways This Verse is Translated:

Cross-References:

Verse

Notes:

Verse Reflection

Reflection

What does this teach me about the Lord?

What does this teach me about Mankind?

Personal Reflection

What is the Lord teaching me?

How can I apply this to my life?

IT'S ALL ABOUT JESUS

Verse Mapping

Context

Who wrote it?
_____

When?
_____

Who to?
_____

Why?
_____
_____
_____

My Paraphrse

_____
_____
_____
_____
_____
_____
_____

Another Translation

_____
_____
_____
_____
_____
_____
_____

Word Study

Definition:
_____
_____
_____
_____

Hebrew/Greek/Aramaic Definition:
_____
_____
_____
_____

Other Ways This Verse is Translated:
_____
_____
_____
_____

Cross-References:
_____
_____
_____
_____

Verse
_____
_____
_____
_____
_____

Notes:
_____
_____
_____
_____
_____
_____
_____
_____
_____
_____

Verse Reflection

Reflection

What does this teach me about the Lord?	What does this teach me about Mankind?

Personal Reflection

What is the Lord teaching me?	How can I apply this to my life?

IT'S ALL ABOUT JESUS

Word Studies

Key Words Study Log

Date	Key Word	Scripture

Key Word Study

Key Verse:

Definition from Standard Dictionary:

Definition from Bible Dictionary:

Scripture References:

Synonyms in Other Bible Translations:

Significance in Original Language:

Summary of What You Learned:

IT'S ALL ABOUT JESUS

Key Word Study

Key Verse:

Definition from Standard Dictionary:

Definition from Bible Dictionary:

Scripture References:

Synonyms in Other Bible Translations:

Significance in Original Language:

Summary of What You Learned:

IT'S ALL ABOUT JESUS

Key Word Study

Key Verse:

Definition from Standard Dictionary:

Definition from Bible Dictionary:

Scripture References:

Synonyms in Other Bible Translations:

Significance in Original Language:

Summary of What You Learned:

IT'S ALL ABOUT JESUS

Key Word Study

Key Verse:

Definition from Standard Dictionary:

Definition from Bible Dictionary:

Scripture References:

Synonyms in Other Bible Translations:

Significance in Original Language:

Summary of What You Learned:

IT'S ALL ABOUT JESUS

Key Word Study

Key Verse:

Definition from Standard Dictionary:

Definition from Bible Dictionary:

Scripture References:

Synonyms in Other Bible Translations:

Significance in Original Language:

Summary of What You Learned:

IT'S ALL ABOUT JESUS

Key Word Study

Key Verse:

Definition from Standard Dictionary:

Definition from Bible Dictionary:

Scripture References:

Synonyms in Other Bible Translations:

Significance in Original Language:

Summary of What You Learned:

IT'S ALL ABOUT JESUS

Key Word Study

Key Verse:

Definition from Standard Dictionary:

Definition from Bible Dictionary:

Scripture References:

Synonyms in Other Bible Translations:

Significance in Original Language:

Summary of What You Learned:

IT'S ALL ABOUT JESUS

Key Word Study

Key Verse:

Definition from Standard Dictionary:

Definition from Bible Dictionary:

Scripture References:

Synonyms in Other Bible Translations:

Significance in Original Language:

Summary of What You Learned:

IT'S ALL ABOUT JESUS

Key Word Study

Key Verse:

Definition from Standard Dictionary:

Definition from Bible Dictionary:

Scripture References:

Synonyms in Other Bible Translations:

Significance in Original Language:

Summary of What You Learned:

Key Word Study

Key Verse:

Definition from Standard Dictionary:

Definition from Bible Dictionary:

Scripture References:

Synonyms in Other Bible Translations:

Significance in Original Language:

Summary of What You Learned:

IT'S ALL ABOUT JESUS

Key Word Study

Key Verse:

Definition from Standard Dictionary:

Definition from Bible Dictionary:

Scripture References:

Synonyms in Other Bible Translations:

Significance in Original Language:

Summary of What You Learned:

IT'S ALL ABOUT JESUS

Key Word Study

Key Verse:

Definition from Standard Dictionary:

Definition from Bible Dictionary:

Scripture References:

Synonyms in Other Bible Translations:

Significance in Original Language:

Summary of What You Learned:

IT'S ALL ABOUT JESUS

Character Studies

Character Study Log

Date	Character	Key Scripture

Character Study

Bio:

Name:

Name Meaning:

Family:

Where Lived:

Time period:

Key Life Events/Details:

How God Used Him/Her:

Key Scripture

Biblical Truths in His/Her Life:

Strengths

Weaknesses

Character Study

Bio:

Name:

Name Meaning:

Family:

Where Lived:

Time period:

Key Scripture

Key Life Events/Details:

Biblical Truths in His/Her Life:

How God Used Him/Her:

Strengths

Weaknesses

IT'S ALL ABOUT JESUS

Character Study

Bio:

Name:

Name Meaning:

Family:

Where Lived:

Time period:

Key Scripture

_____
_____
_____
_____
_____

Key Life Events/Details:

_____
_____
_____
_____
_____
_____
_____
_____
_____
_____

Biblical Truths in His/Her Life:

_____
_____
_____
_____
_____
_____
_____

How God Used Him/Her:

_____
_____
_____
_____
_____
_____
_____
_____

Strengths

Weaknesses

IT'S ALL ABOUT JESUS

Character Study

Bio:

Name:

Name Meaning:

Family:

Where Lived:

Time period:

Key Scripture

Key Life Events/Details:

Biblical Truths in His/Her Life:

Strengths

How God Used Him/Her:

Weaknesses

IT'S ALL ABOUT JESUS

Character Study

Bio:

Name:

Name Meaning:

Family:

Where Lived:

Time period:

Key Life Events/Details:

How God Used Him/Her:

Key Scripture

Biblical Truths in His/Her Life:

Strengths

Weaknesses

Character Study

Bio:

Name:

Name Meaning:

Family:

Where Lived:

Time period:

Key Scripture

Key Life Events/Details:

Biblical Truths in His/Her Life:

How God Used Him/Her:

Strengths

Weaknesses

IT'S ALL ABOUT JESUS

Character Study

Bio:

Name:

Name Meaning:

Family:

Where Lived:

Time period:

Key Scripture

Key Life Events/Details:

Biblical Truths in His/Her Life:

How God Used Him/Her:

Strengths

Weaknesses

Character Study

Bio:

Name:

Name Meaning:

Family:

Where Lived:

Time period:

Key Scripture

_____
_____
_____
_____
_____

Key Life Events/Details:

_____
_____
_____
_____
_____
_____
_____
_____
_____

Biblical Truths in His/Her Life:

_____
_____
_____
_____
_____
_____

Strengths

How God Used Him/Her:

_____
_____
_____
_____
_____
_____
_____
_____

Weaknesses

IT'S ALL ABOUT JESUS

Character Study

Bio:

Name:

Name Meaning:

Family:

Where Lived:

Time period:

Key Scripture

Key Life Events/Details:

Biblical Truths in His/Her Life:

How God Used Him/Her:

Strengths

Weaknesses

IT'S ALL ABOUT JESUS

Character Study

Bio:

Name:

Name Meaning:

Family:

Where Lived:

Time period:

Key Life Events/Details:

_____
_____
_____
_____
_____
_____
_____
_____
_____
_____
_____
_____
_____
_____

How God Used Him/Her:

_____
_____
_____
_____
_____
_____
_____
_____
_____
_____
_____
_____

Key Scripture

_____
_____
_____
_____

Biblical Truths in His/Her Life:

_____
_____
_____
_____
_____
_____
_____

Strengths

Weaknesses

IT'S ALL ABOUT JESUS

Character Study

Bio:

Name:

Name Meaning:

Family:

Where Lived:

Time period:

Key Scripture

Key Life Events/Details:

Biblical Truths in His/Her Life:

How God Used Him/Her:

Strengths

Weaknesses

Character Study

Bio:

Name:

Name Meaning:

Family:

Where Lived:

Time period:

Key Scripture

_____
_____
_____
_____
_____

Key Life Events/Details:

_____
_____
_____
_____
_____
_____
_____
_____
_____
_____
_____
_____

Biblical Truths in His/Her Life:

_____
_____
_____
_____
_____
_____
_____

Strengths

How God Used Him/Her:

_____
_____
_____
_____
_____
_____
_____
_____
_____
_____

Weaknesses

IT'S ALL ABOUT JESUS

Gratitude

Gratefulness log

Date	What I am grateful for:

Gratitude Journal

A few little things:
- _____
- _____
- _____
- _____

The best thing that happened in the last 24 hours:
_____

The most important thing in my life right now is:

Things I've taken for granted:
_____

Someone I am grateful for:

Gratitude Journal

A few little things:
- _____
- _____
- _____
- _____

The best thing that happened in the last 24 hours:
_____

The most important thing in my life right now is:

Things I've taken for granted:
_____

Someone I am grateful for:

IT'S ALL ABOUT JESUS

Gratitude Journal

A few little things:
- _____
- _____
- _____
- _____

The best thing that happened in the last 24 hours:
_____

The most important thing in my life right now is:

Things I've taken for granted:
_____

Someone I am grateful for:

Gratitude Journal

A few little things:
- _____
- _____
- _____
- _____

The best thing that happened in the last 24 hours:
_____

The most important thing in my life right now is:

Things I've taken for granted:
_____

Someone I am grateful for:

IT'S ALL ABOUT JESUS

Gratitude Journal

A few little things:
- _____
- _____
- _____
- _____

The best thing that happened in the last 24 hours:
_____
_____
_____
_____
_____
_____
_____
_____
_____
_____
_____
_____

The most important thing in my life right now is:

Things I've taken for granted:
_____
_____
_____
_____
_____
_____
_____
_____
_____
_____
_____
_____

Someone I am grateful for:

Gratitude Journal

A few little things:
- _____
- _____
- _____
- _____

The best thing that happened in the last 24 hours:
_____

The most important thing in my life right now is:

Things I've taken for granted:
_____

Someone I am grateful for:

IT'S ALL ABOUT JESUS

Gratitude Journal

A few little things:
- _____
- _____
- _____
- _____

The best thing that happened in the last 24 hours:
_____

The most important thing in my life right now is:

Things I've taken for granted:
_____

Someone I am grateful for:

Gratitude Journal

A few little things:
- _____
- _____
- _____

The best thing that happened in the last 24 hours:
_____
_____
_____
_____
_____
_____
_____
_____
_____
_____
_____
_____

The most important thing in my life right now is:

Things I've taken for granted:
_____
_____
_____
_____
_____
_____
_____
_____
_____
_____

Someone I am grateful for:

IT'S ALL ABOUT JESUS

Gratitude Journal

A few little things:
- _____
- _____
- _____
- _____

The best thing that happened in the last 24 hours:
_____
_____
_____
_____
_____
_____
_____
_____
_____
_____
_____
_____

The most important thing in my life right now is:

Things I've taken for granted:
_____
_____
_____
_____
_____
_____
_____
_____
_____
_____

Someone I am grateful for:

Gratitude Journal

A few little things:
- _____
- _____
- _____

The best thing that happened in the last 24 hours:
_____
_____
_____
_____
_____
_____
_____
_____
_____
_____

The most important thing in my life right now is:

Things I've taken for granted:
_____
_____
_____
_____
_____
_____
_____
_____
_____

Someone I am grateful for:

IT'S ALL ABOUT JESUS

Gratitude Journal

A few little things:
- _____
- _____
- _____
- _____

The best thing that happened in the last 24 hours:
_____

The most important thing in my life right now is:

Things I've taken for granted:
_____

Someone I am grateful for:

Gratitude Journal

A few little things:
- _____
- _____
- _____
- _____

The best thing that happened in the last 24 hours:
_____
_____
_____
_____
_____
_____
_____
_____
_____
_____
_____
_____

The most important thing in my life right now is:

Things I've taken for granted:
_____
_____
_____
_____
_____
_____
_____
_____
_____

Someone I am grateful for:

IT'S ALL ABOUT JESUS

Forgiveness

Forgiveness log

Date	Who or what do I need to forgive?

Forgiveness log

Date	Who or what do I need to forgive?

Miracles

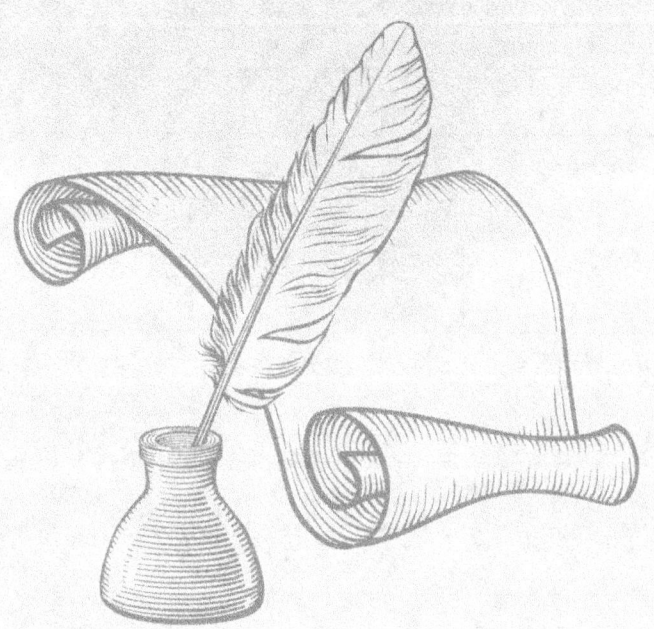

Miracles log

Date	Where it happened	Description of miracle:

Miracles log

Date	Where it happened	Description of miracle:

My "Go-To" Scripture

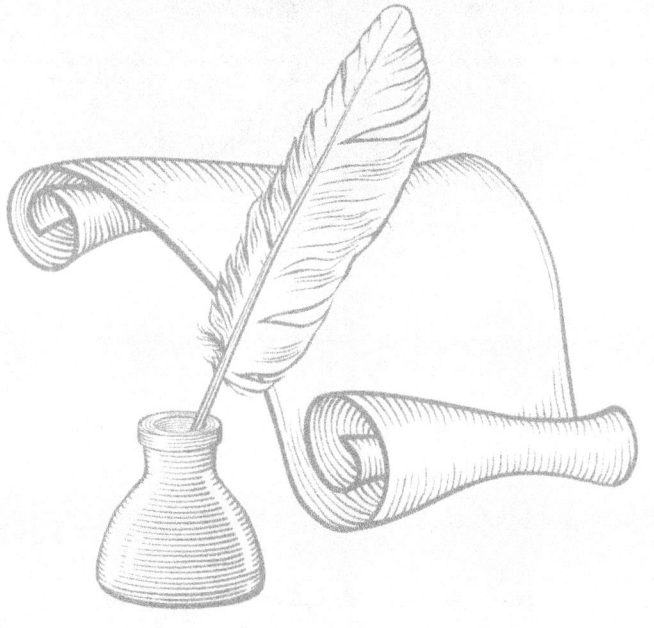

My "Go-To" Scripture Lists

Topic:	Topic:

Topic:	Topic:

Topic:	Topic:

IT'S ALL ABOUT JESUS

My "Go-To" Scripture lists

Topic:

Topic:

Topic:

Topic:

Topic:

Topic:

IT'S ALL ABOUT JESUS

My Favorite Verses

My Favorite Bible Verses

Passage:

Passage:

Passage:

Passage:

Passage:

Passage:

Passage:

Passage:

My Favorite Bible Verses

Passage:
_____
_____
_____
_____
_____

Passage:
_____
_____
_____
_____
_____

Passage:
_____
_____
_____
_____
_____

Passage:
_____
_____
_____
_____
_____

Passage:
_____
_____
_____
_____
_____

Passage:
_____
_____
_____
_____
_____

Passage:
_____
_____
_____
_____
_____

Passage:
_____
_____
_____
_____
_____

IT'S ALL ABOUT JESUS

Additional Notes

Additional Notes

IT'S ALL ABOUT JESUS

Additional Notes

About the Author

Melissa grew up with a passion for learning and for studying the Bible. Over the years, she had discovered a wide range of techniques for developing and deepening her Bible studies. Although there are a lot of approaches available, she discovered that none of them really tied everything together or permitted people to adopt the same approaches depending on where they were in their relationship with the Lord. After hearing about other people's struggles with Bible studying and journal keeping, she was inspired to help them. She wanted to show that studying the Bible does not have to be intimidating or difficult, and that such studies do not have to take on the same format as traditional journaling. So she designed this Bible journal with the belief that those who use it will come to know the Lord, grow in Him, gain understanding of His Word, and allowing their lives to be transformed.

Currently residing in Arizona with her husband Greg and son Kenneth, Melissa is Littleton, Colorado native who served in the US Air Force. She and her spouse ar involved in ministry together and own a company called By the Bootstraps. Her husban also a US Air Force veteran, was just ordained as a chaplain, so she anticipates that th Lord will provide more opportunities for them to serve together and carry out H purpose for them.

By The Bootstraps ©